T0114075

'When working with dyscalculia the questions from teaching staff and parents are commonly – "how do we know?" "what's the difference between maths anxiety and dyscalculia?" and "what do we do?" As we learn more with regard to assisting dyscalculic learners to achieve their goals, the demand for a text of this type increases dramatically. Judy's book is definitely not a "shelf sitter", the text is written in an easy to read, progressive and practical manner. The descriptions and expansions of terms and phrases are fantastic, the "how to" chapters on learning environments and resources can be seamlessly incorporated into lessons. A section on useful websites and publications has real value in highlighting respected information sources'.

> – **Gary Sharpe**, Learning challenges with numbers, Dyscalculia – New Zealand

'The book's greatest strength may be its clear overview of dyscalculia as a core number sense deficit, distinguishing it from difficulties in mathematics in general. The author provides essential advice, practical guide and updated recourses to experts, school teachers and parents on dealing with dyscalculia in terms of early identification, diagnosis and intervention'.

> – **Giannis Karagiannakis**, Fellow researcher, University of Athens

'*All About Dyscalculia* is an invaluable practical and comprehensive guide for all those working with early years and primary age pupils who struggle with numeracy. It explains thoroughly the meaning and implications of dyscalculia in the classroom, when those with this condition have neuro-atypical brains. Practical guidance is extensive, about appropriate multisensory methods of assisting pupils' development of "number sense", that is, common sense about the quantities of number values and how they can perform calculations with understanding. Pupils in difficulty can come to understand number work, rather than just being "taught" and this is clearly explained. This information-packed book is also suitable for more experienced practitioners, with discussion and extensive referencing, for further study of this little-known specific condition. I thoroughly recommend it and learnt more about luminaries in this field too, such as the Hungarian mathematician George Polya, known as "The Father of Problem Solving"'.

– **Jane Emerson**, Speech and Language Therapist, Specialist Literacy and Numeracy Teacher, and founder of Emerson House Learning Centre, London

'Dyscalculia is a developmental disability that is present from the early years, but this may not be immediately apparent to parents and educators. How can we identify dyscalculic learners early, and how can we best support them? This book answers these burning questions and more. Readers will not only learn about the typical milestones of mathematics development, and the early warning signs of dyscalculia, but they will also receive essential practical guidance on how to proceed from there. The book also addresses many other important topics, including how to best explain dyscalculia to parents, and how to prepare struggling learners to transition to secondary school. From debunking the myths around dyscalculia to improving the mathematical vocabulary of learners, this well-researched and insightful book provides highly practical guidance to educators who want to offer the best possible support to struggling learners'.

– **Kinga Morsanyi**, Senior Lecturer in Mathematical Cognition, Loughborough University

ALL ABOUT DYSCALCULIA

All About Dyscalculia is an accessible and informative guide for primary school teachers, designed to increase their knowledge and understanding of dyscalculia and provide practical strategies and advice to build the self-esteem and motivation of learners in their care.

The book explores the indicators of dyscalculia, before detailing a range of teaching strategies that will support dyscalculic children and help them to develop their mathematical understanding and resilience. Throughout the book, there is an emphasis on creating an empathetic learning ethos in the classroom and school that will minimise maths anxiety and lead to a more positive outcome for all learners. *All About Dyscalculia* includes:

- A comprehensive introduction to dyscalculia and steps to help teachers identify learners with dyscalculia in their classrooms.
- Practical strategies for building specific maths abilities, as well as broader problem-solving skills.
- Advice for teachers and parents on how to reduce maths anxiety and support the development of maths proficiency in learners.
- Easy to dip in and out of chapters with worked examples make this book accessible to all teachers and parents.

With suggestions for immediate impact, as well as ideas for more detailed interventions, this practical book will be essential reading for all mainstream primary teachers and SENCOs, as well as a helpful guide to supporting children with dyscalculia at home.

Judy Hornigold is an educational consultant specialising in maths and learners with dyscalculia and dyslexia. Her teaching career started in primary schools before she moved into teaching children with special needs. Judy delivers key notes, workshops and training in Dyscalculia and Maths Mastery across the world, including New Zealand, Australia and Dubai. She has been involved in curriculum development for the past ten years and co-founded the Dyscalculia Association in 2018, where she runs training courses for teachers on dyscalculia.

All About SEND
Series Advisor: Natalie Packer

All About SEND provides busy teachers and SENCOs with essential guidance and practical strategies to effectively support learner with special educational needs and disabilities. Each accessible and informative book focuses on a common area of need and explores key traits and terminology, debunks myths and misconceptions, and introduces readers to a range of easy-to-implement ideas for practice and concrete solutions to everyday challenges.

ALL ABOUT AUTISM
A Practical Guide for Primary Teachers
Lynn McCann

ALL ABOUT AUTISM
A Practical Guide for Secondary Teachers
Lynn McCann

ALL ABOUT DYSCALCULIA
A Practical Guide for Primary Teachers
Judy Hornigold

ALL ABOUT DYSCALCULIA

A PRACTICAL GUIDE FOR PRIMARY TEACHERS

Judy Hornigold

Routledge
Taylor & Francis Group

LONDON AND NEW YORK

Designed cover image: © Getty Images

First published 2024
by Routledge
4 Park Square, Milton Park, Abingdon, Oxon OX14 4RN

and by Routledge
605 Third Avenue, New York, NY 10158

Routledge is an imprint of the Taylor & Francis Group, an informa business

British Library Cataloguing-in-Publication Data
A catalogue record for this book is available from the British Library

ISBN: 978-1-032-35381-4 (hbk)
ISBN: 978-1-032-35382-1 (pbk)
ISBN: 978-1-003-32662-5 (ebk)

DOI: 10.4324/9781003326625

Typeset in Interstate
by Deanta Global Publishing Services, Chennai, India

CONTENTS

Foreword **viii**
Preface **xi**

PART 1
INTRODUCTION TO DYSCALCULIA 1

1   Introduction to dyscalculia   3
2   Maths anxiety   13
3   Indicators of dyscalculia   23
4   Debunking the myths   29

PART 2
PRACTICAL STRATEGIES 33

5   The typical developmental stages of maths in EYFS
     and Key Stage 1   35
6   Good practice   44
7   Specific strategies for Early Years and Key Stage 1   71
8   Specific strategies for Key Stage 2   96
9   Working with parents   109
10   Planning for transition   117
11   Further resources   119

Index **131**

FOREWORD

All teachers are teachers of learners with special educational needs and disabilities (SEND). Those professionals who work in truly inclusive schools will understand that SEND is everyone's responsibility. However, the situation has not always been like this. When I started my teaching career 30 years ago, learners who had additional needs were more likely to be seen as the responsibility of the Special Educational Needs Coordinator (SENCO). As the person in school who 'held' the SEND knowledge and expertise, the SENCO would often be a lone force in championing, and meeting, the needs of this particular group of learners.

The picture in education is somewhat different today. The profile of the children and young people we teach continues to change; the impact of the COVID-19 pandemic, for example, has led to an increase in those identified with gaps in their learning, or with mental health concerns. The number of learners with complex needs being educated within mainstream schools also continues to rise. As professionals, we now have a greater awareness and understanding of some of the challenges our learners face and, as a result, are more determined to do our best to support them to achieve. We understand that this cannot be the role of one person – the SENCO – alone. Every teacher needs to be a teacher of SEND.

Teaching learners with SEND may be one of the most rewarding things you ever do in your classroom. When you observe a learner who has really struggled to grasp a new idea or concept finally achieve their 'lightbulb moment', it's all the more sweeter knowing the amount of effort they had put in to get there. However, teaching learners with SEND can also be one of the most challenging aspects of your career. In a 2019 survey[1] carried out by the Department for Education (DfE) in England, the level of confidence amongst teachers in supporting learners with SEND was reported as very low. Relevant professional development in this area is, at best, patchy; only 41% of the teachers surveyed by the DfE felt there was sufficient SEND training in place for all teachers.

So how do we overcome this challenge? Evidence suggests that the best place to start is through the delivery of inclusive, High Quality Teaching (HQT). As the Education Endowment Foundation (EEF) report[2] tells us, there is no 'magic bullet' for teaching learners with SEND and to a great extent, good teaching for those with SEND is good teaching for all. This means we need to develop a repertoire of effective teaching strategies such as scaffolding, explicit instruction and use of technology, then use these strategies flexibly to meet the needs of individuals or groups of learners.

Although a focus on effective HQT in the classroom is the starting point, some learners will require more specific teaching methods to meet their individual needs. There is no substitute for really getting to know a child or young person so you can fully understand their personal strengths, potential barriers to learning and what works for them in the classroom. However, it can still be helpful for us as professionals to develop a more general understanding of some of the common areas of need we are likely to come across and to have a range of strategies we can try implementing within our practice. This is where *All About SEND* can help.

The *All About SEND* series of books aims to support every teacher to be a teacher of SEND. Each book has been designed to enable teachers, and other professionals such as support staff, to develop their knowledge and understanding of how to effectively promote teaching and learning for those with identified areas of need. The books provide essential information and a range of practical strategies for supporting learners in the classroom. Written by expert practitioners, the guidance has been informed by a wealth of first-hand experience, with the views of children and young people with SEND and their parents taking centre stage.

This book, *All About Dyscalculia: Supporting Children with Dyscalculia in the Primary School*, focuses on supporting learners who struggle with maths. It is authored by Judy Hornigold, an educational consultant specialising in specific learning difficulties. Her passion for empowering teachers to rethink the way they teach maths to support all learners to enjoy maths and become competent mathematicians is evident throughout the book. *All About Dyscalculia: Supporting Children with Dyscalculia in the Primary School* provides a wealth of information on the research and theories behind dyscalculia, along with a range of practical strategies for teachers to apply in the classroom.

Thank you for choosing to read this book and for embracing the challenge of responsibility: every teacher a teacher of SEND.

Natalie Packer
SEND Consultant, Director of NPEC Ltd.
@NataliePacker

NOTES

1 https://assets.publishing.service.gov.uk/government/uploads/system/uploads/attachment_data/file/1063620/SEND_review_right_support_right_place_right_time_accessible.pdf. p. 42.
2 https://educationendowmentfoundation.org.uk/education-evidence/guidance-reports/send.

PREFACE

I had mixed experiences of learning maths at school. There was one teacher in particular who clearly didn't enjoy teaching maths and I suspect wasn't that fond of children either! Her answer to any question was, 'it is common sense', and I was left feeling that maths was an inaccessible subject and one that I would never be able to master or enjoy. Happily, before too much damage was done, she was replaced by Mrs Robyn. Mrs Robyn loved maths! Her enthusiasm for the subject radiated from every pore of her body and before long I was hooked. I was a maths convert. Her incredible teaching changed everything for me and instilled in me a lifelong passion for maths. After all these years I still find it endlessly fascinating, often breathtakingly beautiful and always full of surprises. It was then inevitable that I would end up doing maths as my degree subject at Nottingham University and I subsequently embarked upon a career as a chartered accountant. However, this was short-lived as I had always wanted to teach. At primary school age, I would 'teach' my teddy bears and could think of nothing that I would rather do. So, after a few years in the world of accountancy, I retrained as a primary school teacher and never looked back. A career break to have my children followed and then when my youngest was around 6 years old, we discovered that he was dyslexic. This led me to retrain as a dyslexia specialist and eventually I became a senior lecturer at Edgehill University, where I worked on their dyslexia specialist teaching programme. It occurred to me then that there was quite a lot of provision for dyslexia, but very little for learners who struggled with maths. Consequently, I was instrumental in developing a PGCE in Dyscalculia. This was followed by a collaboration with Steve

Chinn, when we set up the Dyscalculia Association in 2018 and later our online Level 5 Dyscalculia course. Over the years, I have seen many teachers rethink the way that they teach maths and there is now, thankfully, more awareness and support for learners with dyscalculia. However, we still have a long way to go, and I hope that this book will go some way to continuing to improve teacher knowledge and skills as well as improving the outcomes for so many of our learners who struggle with maths.

Part 1

INTRODUCTION TO DYSCALCULIA

INTRODUCTION TO DYSCALCULIA

WHAT IS DYSCALCULIA?

This sounds like a simple question, but the reality is far more complex. There is still a lot that we don't know about dyscalculia and much debate about its definition.

Dyscalculia is generally thought of as a specific learning difficulty in mathematics, or, more particularly, arithmetic. The word 'dyscalculia' has both Greek and Latin roots and literally means 'counting badly': the Greek prefix 'dys' means badly and the Latin 'calculare' means 'to count'.

In 2019 the British Dyslexia Association (BDA) put forward their definition of dyscalculia, which was devised by the BDA Dyscalculia Committee.

> *Dyscalculia is a specific and persistent difficulty in understanding arithmetic and basic number sense. It may also affect retrieval of number facts and key procedures, fluent calculation, and interpreting numerical information. It is diverse in character and occurs across all ages and abilities. Dyscalculia is an unexpected difficulty in maths that cannot be explained by external factors.*
>
> *Mathematics difficulties are best thought of as a continuum, not a distinct category, with dyscalculia at the extreme end of this continuum. It should be expected that Developmental Dyscalculia will be distinguishable from general mathematical difficulties due to the severity of difficulties with symbolic and non-symbolic magnitude, number sense and subitising.*

DOI: 10.4324/9781003326625-2

Definitions are not easy to write and our first attempt ran to two sides of A4 paper. We clearly needed to make it more succinct and I think it would be beneficial to dig a bit deeper to explore exactly what this definition is all about.

WHAT DOES THIS DEFINITION ACTUALLY MEAN?

> *Dyscalculia is a specific and persistent difficulty in understanding arithmetic and basic number sense.*

Dyscalculia is a specific learning difference. Put simply, the brains of people with dyscalculia are wired differently. It is an example of one of many neuro-diversities that exist in the human population.

It is primarily associated with a lack of understanding of our number system and the four operations: addition, subtraction, multiplication and division.

The definition also refers to number sense, which goes beyond a basic understanding of our number system and the four operations. People with good number sense will not only understand the effect of the four operations in maths, but will also be flexible in their approach to numbers. They will estimate an answer and will be alerted to any answers that are not reasonable based on their estimate. Good number sense also involves the ability to compare numbers and to appreciate different levels of magnitude; for example, knowing that 1 billion is substantially larger than 1 million.

Other examples of good number sense include:

- Understanding concepts such as more or less.
- Understanding our place value system: base-10.
- Matching the number symbol to the numerical quantity. In other words, having a mental image of five objects when presented with the symbol 5.
- Being able to round to an appropriate degree of accuracy.
- Looking for connections; for example, if $5 + 6 = 11$, then $11 - 5 = 6$ and $50 + 60 = 110$

- Finding efficient ways of working; for example, when calculating $6,000 \times 0.25$, using the method of halving 6,000 and halving again to give 1,500, rather than doing a long multiplication.

Professor Mahesh Sharma states that

> Number sense is the flexible use of number relationships and making sense of numerical information in various contexts. Learners with good number sense can represent and use a number in multiple ways depending on the context and purpose. In computations and operations, they can decompose and recompose numbers with ease and fluency.

Learners with good number sense are effectively accessing a much easier version of maths, they can apply efficient, elegant and effective strategies, such as halving and halving again to find a quarter, rather than multiplying by 0.25. Conversely, learners with poor number sense are working at a very procedural level, applying longwinded algorithms when there are simpler, more relational ways to approach the maths. Not only are they finding maths difficult, but they are also doing a much harder version of the subject.

> *It may also affect retrieval of number facts and key procedures, fluent calculation, and interpreting numerical information.*

People with dyscalculia will find it very difficult to recall basic number facts as they have not attached any numerical meaning to the numerical symbols.

For example, when thinking about 6×7, they are not visualising six groups of seven, or using their knowledge of 6×6 to work out 6×7. For a person with dyscalculia, who has not associated numerical magnitude to a numerical symbol, the task is akin to learning that $A \times Y = P$ or that $B \times M = J$. Imagine having

100 of these letter combinations to remember, with no sense of what the letters represent; then it is easy to see just how demanding a task this would be.

Fluent calculation refers to our ability to look at the calculation and use our number sense to simplify it, or to even just do it mentally.

For example, 39+40+41 could be thought of as 3×40, rather than as a column addition. If we know that 3×4=12, then we can make the connection that 3×40 must be 120.

> *It is diverse in character and occurs across all ages and abilities.*

No two dyscalculic people will present in exactly the same way, and it is very common for dyscalculic people to have co-occurring learning differences such as dyslexia or dyspraxia. Some learners with dyscalculia may also have difficulty with their short-term, working or long-term memory. Some may have difficulty with spatial awareness. Dyscalculia is not more prevalent in one gender than another and is a condition that is lifelong and present from birth.

Some researchers refer to primary and secondary dyscalculia. Primary dyscalculia is a 'within child' difference, attributed to the neurodiversity of that individual. Secondary dyscalculia is associated with maths difficulties caused by external factors, such as poor teaching or missed schooling. For the purposes of this book, I will be referring to primary dyscalculia, following on from the definition that states:

> *Dyscalculia is an unexpected difficulty in maths that cannot be explained by external factors.*
>
> *Mathematics difficulties are best thought of as a continuum, not a distinct category, with dyscalculia at the extreme end of this continuum.*

It can be difficult sometimes to see where general maths difficulties end and dyscalculia begins, as there is often an overlap between the two. People with dyscalculia may also be affected by external factors. We need to be careful here not to lump all learners with maths difficulties into the category of dyscalculia. Understanding the root cause of the difficulties in maths is key to being able to develop effective strategies for support and intervention.

> *It should be expected that Developmental Dyscalculia will be distinguishable from general mathematical difficulties due to the severity of difficulties with symbolic and non-symbolic magnitude, number sense and subitising.*

SYMBOLIC AND NON-SYMBOLIC MAGNITUDE

Any screening tool for dyscalculia will include tests of symbolic and non-symbolic magnitude comparison. These generally have a stroop effect included. In this type of test, the learner will be asked to identify the larger number out of a pair of numbers.

In a congruent pair, the numerically larger number is also physically larger. Dyscalculic people perform at the same level as non-dyscalculic people on this task. In an incongruent pair, the numerically larger number is physically smaller, and this is the stroop effect. Learners with dyscalculia will automatically attach the physical size of the number and disregard the numerical magnitude as they have not made the connection between the numerical symbol and its numerical magnitude. This stroop test is a very good way of identifying learners with dyscalculia as there is a marked difference in performance between dyscalculic and non-dyscalculic people.

Congruent pair	Incongruent pair	Neutral pair – Numerical task	Neutral pair- Physical task

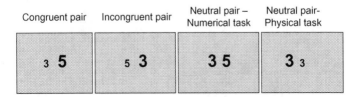

Non-symbolic magnitude comparison is commonly assessed using dot arrays, or pictures of groups of objects.

SUBITISING

Subitising is our ability to immediately recognise how many items are in a set without counting them. It is an instantaneous response and typically we can subitise around five items that are randomly arranged.

There are two types of subitising.

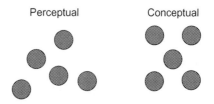

Perceptual subitising is instant recognition of quantity where the items are randomly arranged.

Conceptual subitising is instant recognition of quantity where the items are arranged in a pattern.

Typically, we can perceptually subitise up to five or maybe six items.

For conceptual subitising, we can recognise larger amounts as we are using our pattern knowledge and also simple addition facts.

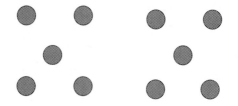

Looking at this image we can readily see that there are ten dots, as we have recognised two sets of five dots and have mentally added them together to give ten.

Conceptual subitising is one of the ways that we help learners with dyscalculia to attach numerical magnitude to a numerical symbol. The use of familiar dot patterns will help with automatic recognition of quantity and then that image can be linked to the numerical symbol.

WHAT CAUSES DYSCALCULIA?

There is still a great deal of research that is ongoing in this area and the causes of dyscalculia are yet to be fully understood.

GENETICS

Studies have shown that a learner with dyscalculia often has a sibling, parent or other close relative with similar mathematical difficulties. Dyscalculia can therefore be hereditary, though the parents are very unlikely to have been diagnosed with the condition.

BRAIN DIFFERENCES

MRI scans have shown that there is reduced grey matter in the parietal lobes and the occipital, temporal and frontal parts of the brain. The parietal lobe areas are central to the processing of numbers and calculation. The frontal lobe areas are used for recall of numerical facts and also for working memory.

PRENATAL INFLUENCES

There is evidence linking dyscalculia with exposure to alcohol in the womb. Prematurity and low birth weight can also be contributing factors.

Turner's syndrome, Fragile X syndrome, Velocardiofacial syndrome and Williams syndrome are some of the genetic disorders that have been observed in people with dyscalculia.

BRAIN INJURY

Dyscalculia may be caused by a brain injury, and is then referred to as acquired dyscalculia. There was a case of a man who had suffered a trauma to the brain that had caused him to lose all symbolic knowledge in maths. He was unable to calculate 2 + 2, unless it was written in words. He could do the calculation when presented as 'two plus two' and give the answer 'four'.

WORKING MEMORY

Working memory plays a large part in mental addition as well as planning and organisation. So, poor working memory could cause many of the difficulties seen in learners with dyscalculia.

MATHS ANXIETY

Prolonged and severe anxiety around maths can also lead to learners appearing as though they are dyscalculic, when in reality it is the debilitating fear that is causing their issues with maths. Their anxiety is so great that they are unable to tackle any maths at all. Maths anxiety is a huge issue in schools and the wider community. It is believed that around 20–25% of learners have experienced maths anxiety at some stage and it can start in primary school, sometimes even in Key Stage 1.

Chapter 2 of this book explores maths anxiety in more detail.

THE IMPACT OF DYSCALCULIA

IN SCHOOL

Maths is a subject that can't be avoided in school and if a learner has dyscalculia that has not been recognised or supported then the impact can be severe. Learners may develop the notion that they will never be able to do maths, or that they are stupid. This can have a detrimental effect on their self-esteem and their mental well-being and, if left unaddressed, could impact on other areas of the curriculum and their attitude to learning in general. All too often problems with maths in secondary school stem from undiagnosed or unsupported difficulties in primary school so it is vital that difficulties with maths and dyscalculia are identified and ameliorated as soon as possible.

IN LATER LIFE

The impact of dyscalculia is far-reaching and can have a profound impact on daily life, especially in the workplace, where people may be asked to perform mathematical tasks without prior warning and the opportunity for preparation. It can have a severe impact on job prospects and promotional opportunities for those in work.

Some dyscalculic adults never learn to drive, because of the numerical demands of driving and map reading (although SAT NAVs can help a great deal here). This means that they have to rely on public transport, and could have issues in terms of reading timetables, which can be very challenging for people with dyscalculia.

Dyscalculia can also lead to social isolation, due to an inability to be at the right place at the right time or to understand the rules and scoring systems of games and sports.

Personal finances and budgeting will also be an issue for people with dyscalculia. Research shows that adults with low numeracy earn on average £2,100 less per annum than adults with average or above average numeracy.

To have dyscalculia can be a very frustrating experience, but it does not mean that you will never achieve in life. It is, after all, a *specific* learning difficulty. Paul Moorcraft's book *It Just Doesn't Add Up* is testament to what can be achieved despite having severe dyscalculia. Surprisingly, a number of mathematics professors could be described as dyscalculic, reminding us that this is a specific difficulty with arithmetic and not with every branch of mathematics.

CO-OCCURRING DIFFICULTIES

Whilst dyscalculia may occur in isolation, it is very common for this learning difference to co-occur with other specific learning differences, such as dyslexia and dyspraxia. This can lead to quite complex learning profiles, and it can be hard to identify the root cause of the difficulties that the learner is presenting with. This is particularly true with younger children whose difficulties may be due to developmental delay rather than a specific learning difference. Whilst I would not advocate formal diagnosis and assessment at an early age, it is important to be aware of those children whose development is not typical and not commensurate with their peers. The sooner we can identify any difficulties, the sooner we can put effective interventions in place.

SUMMARY

- Dyscalculia is a specific and persistent difficulty in understanding arithmetic and basic number sense.
- Developmental dyscalculia will be distinguishable from general mathematical difficulties due to the severity of difficulties with symbolic and non-symbolic magnitude, number sense and subitising.
- The causes are varied and not yet fully understood; research is ongoing and much needed.
- The impact of dyscalculia is profound if not identified and supported as soon as possible.

REFERENCES

Moorcraft, P. (2014). *It Just Doesn't Add Up.* Croydon, UK: Filament Publishing.

MATHS ANXIETY

Dyscalculia and maths anxiety go hand in hand and it would be remiss not to focus on the prevalence and impact of maths anxiety on pupil well-being and attainment. Whilst the prevalence of dyscalculia is around 5–8% of the population, a much greater percentage of people struggle with maths anxiety. All too often maths anxiety is overlooked, and the cause of the anxiety is never established. This can have a very detrimental effect on pupil well-being and their belief in their ability to progress in maths.

In some ways, one could argue that maths anxiety is a greater problem than dyscalculia. It certainly affects a larger number of people and is not only found in struggling learners. Some of our high-achieving learners also have maths anxiety. As practitioners, we need to understand the causes of maths anxiety and how to recognise learners who are suffering from maths anxiety. We need to understand the cause in order to support the learner and alleviate their anxiety – sometimes the solution can be very simple and small adjustments to our teaching practice can be hugely beneficial to learners struggling with maths anxiety.

Maths anxiety has been defined as

> a feeling of tension and apprehension that interferes with maths performance ability, the manipulation of numbers and the solving of mathematical problems in a wide variety of ordinary life and academic situations.
>
> (Richardson and Suinn, 1972)

DOI: 10.4324/9781003326625-3

Maths anxiety has also been defined as

> the panic, helplessness, paralysis, and mental disorganization that arises among some people when they are required to solve a mathematical problem.
>
> *(Tobias and Weissbrod, 1980)*

Maths anxiety is surprisingly common but not always recognised or acknowledged. The statistics around levels of anxiety are quite shocking.

MATHS ANXIETY IN LEARNERS

36% of 15-24-year-olds in the UK feel anxious about maths.
10% of 8-13-year-olds suffer from maths anxiety.

These two statistics alone beg the following questions. What is causing 8-year-olds to be anxious about maths? Why are we not recognising and addressing this anxiety?

Why is anxiety increasing as the learners get older?

MATHS ANXIETY IN PARENTS

25% of parents don't feel able to teach their learners basic addition and subtraction without the use of a calculator.
40% of parents would not be able to show their learners how to split a restaurant bill with friends.
Women are twice as anxious as men about maths.

There has been research that suggests that parents are transferring their anxiety to their children, unwittingly, when they try to help them with maths (Maloney et al., 2015).

MATHS ANXIETY IN HIGHER EDUCATION

Only 26% of undergraduate students have the numerical capability needed for daily life and work.

These alarming statistics are taken from *A Guide to Tackling Maths Anxiety* (www.Pearson.com) and make for sobering reading. We can't ignore this problem and need to do more to support learners who are anxious about maths.

A global student survey in 2021, led by Cuemath, found that maths anxiety is higher in the UK than in any of the other 20 countries surveyed, with girls being more stressed by maths than boys. Anxiety levels were found to peak at the age of 14.

Maths anxiety can range in severity from feelings of mild anxiety to a profound and debilitating fear of maths. If not addressed at an early stage the anxiety is very likely to snowball. When we are put in a stressful situation our bodies naturally go into fight or flight mode. Unfortunately, in a classroom situation, we cannot employ either of those responses, so the body produces more adrenalin to make us respond and escape the stress situation. If this experience is repeated many times, it triggers a Pavlovian response where the brain 'learns' to shut down when presented with maths. At this stage it will be almost impossible to teach the child any maths as they are in such a state of anxiety. Learners with this level of maths anxiety may appear to be refusing to do the maths and they may be labelled as being badly behaved, but a much more likely cause for their behaviour is maths anxiety.

SIGNS OF MATHS ANXIETY

Just as the causes of maths anxiety are varied, so are the symptoms. Learners may present with either physical or psychological symptoms or a combination of both.

Physical symptoms include nail- or lip-biting, stomach aches, headaches, nausea, clammy hands, increased heart rate, shortness of breath, fidgeting, sweating, frequent loo visits.

Psychological symptoms include low self-esteem, lack of confidence in their answers, confusion, anxiety, poor concentration, feelings of helplessness, giving up easily and frequently.

You may have learners in your class who respond to maths in one or more of the following ways:

- Not getting started with their work.
- Taking far too much time to complete work.

- Only doing the 'easy' questions.
- Shrugging their shoulders and saying 'I don't know' – without appearing to have even thought about it.
- Being impulsive and blurting out answers.
- Not showing their working.
- Never finishing their work.

If this is the response to maths, then the first approach would be to have a conversation with the child to ascertain if maths anxiety is at the root of this behaviour. Most of the time learners aren't behaving in this way because they are being 'naughty' or 'lazy'. There will be an underlying cause or trigger.

The causes of the anxiety can be very complex or may just be rooted in one particular thing as the following case studies show.

Child A

Child A was displaying high levels of anxiety in class and was very withdrawn and uncommunicative. He failed to complete any given tasks in the lesson.

After a discussion with his teacher, Child A reported that he was terrified of his name being pulled out of the pot of named lolly sticks that the teacher used when asking questions. The teacher removed Child A's stick from the pot and after a couple of weeks the child became more engaged in class and started to attempt written work. At this point the teacher suggested that if Child A wanted to answer a question he could simply raise his hand. The following week, he put his hand up and correctly answered a question in front of his peers. Something that would have been unimaginable just a few weeks before. There are often small triggers that can cause huge anxiety, and the simplest of solutions can have a huge effect on alleviating anxiety and stress.

Child B

Child B was generally well behaved but would often pick a fight with other learners at morning break time. This led to the child being taken to the headteacher's office for the first ten minutes after morning play. Eventually, when this was happening more and more frequently, the teacher investigated what the issue was. The child confessed that they were fearful of the mental maths part of the lesson that always took place in the first ten minutes after morning play. Once this issue was explained then alternative activities were planned, and the child didn't have any more visits to the headteacher.

These case studies demonstrate that sometimes, the solution is relatively simple. If we can find out the cause of the anxiety, then it will be much easier to reduce that anxiety. Sadly, many learners have suffered years of anxiety and it is more ingrained and more difficult to alleviate, which is another reason why we must try to identify it as soon as possible and teach in a way that will lessen the anxiety.

CAUSES OF MATHS ANXIETY

Teachers' attitude and confidence in maths

A 2008 study by Elizabeth Jackson found that 68% of students on a primary teacher training course had a lack of confidence in teaching maths.

The study found that it was their attitude to maths rather than their cognitive ability that was the cause of the anxiety.

Teachers who lack confidence in teaching maths will often teach in a procedural way and this leads to a very superficial understanding of maths. Learners will apply procedures without thought to whether that is the best approach; for example, using a column subtraction to calculate 201 - 199. When taught procedurally, maths becomes a mechanical subject, reliant on automatic recall of many facts, rules and algorithms. If something is forgotten there is no way of reconstructing that knowledge.

As teachers we have a great responsibility in how we convey a subject to our learners. This responsibility was highlighted to me when I was training a group of teachers. One of the teachers worked in adult education and ran a functional maths course in the evenings. He recalled a lady who had come to the course at

78 years of age. He politely asked what had brought her to the course after all this time! She said that she remembered vividly exactly where she was sitting, what she was wearing and even what the weather was like at the moment that her teacher told her (at age ten) that she was too stupid to ever learn maths. This traumatic experience had haunted her for all of her life and she was determined not to leave this world unable to do maths.

Sadly, it is not uncommon for one harsh comment to have a life-long detrimental effect. We would like to think that we are all a bit more enlightened these days and aware of safeguarding learners' mental well-being but we can unwittingly say things that can cause a lot of damage. I have been guilty of this myself. When tutoring a child whom I had worked with over a long period of time, I tried to reassure her that we would do something 'easy' today (she had come to the lesson feeling very anxious and low). Unfortunately, she found my 'easy' task anything but 'easy' and left the lesson feeling worse than when she arrived. It is hard to forgive yourself for these things, and happily all was redeemed the next lesson, but it is an episode that I sincerely regret and will never forget.

TEACHING APPROACHES

Timed tests

Giving timed tests can be one of the biggest triggers of maths anxiety. When we are put under timed pressure it can have a very detrimental effect on our working memory and it is difficult to think clearly. On top of that, many learners with maths learning difficulties and dyscalculia have poor processing speed and it takes them longer to come up with an answer, particularly when doing mental maths. There is a pervading idea that being fast at maths equates with being good at maths and many learners have bought into this notion. In reality, speed has nothing to do with mathematical understanding. While it may be useful to have immediate and automatic recall of your times tables, it doesn't make you a great mathematician – just in the same way that knowing the alphabet off by heart doesn't make you a great author!

To illustrate this irrelevance of speed in maths, let me introduce you to Laurent-Moïse Schwartz (1915-2002). He was a French mathematician who was awarded the Fields Medal in 1950. The Fields Medal in maths is the equivalent of a Nobel Prize. This is what he had to say about his experience at school:

> I was always deeply uncertain about my own intellectual capacity; I thought I was unintelligent. And it is true that I was, and still am, rather slow. I need time to seize things because I always need to understand them fully. Even when I was the first to answer the teacher's questions, I knew it was because they happened to be questions to which I already knew the answer. But if a new question arose, usually students who weren't as good as I was answered before me. Towards the end of eleventh grade, I secretly thought of myself as stupid. I worried about this for a long time. Not only did I believe I was stupid, but I couldn't understand the contradiction between this stupidity and my good grades. I never talked about this to anyone, but I always felt convinced that my imposture would someday be revealed: the whole world and myself would finally see that what looked like intelligence was really just an illusion. If this ever happened, apparently no one noticed it, and I'm still just as slow. When a teacher dictated something to us, I had real trouble taking notes; it's still difficult for me to follow a seminar.
>
> At the end of eleventh grade, I took the measure of the situation, and came to the conclusion that rapidity doesn't have a precise relation to intelligence. What is important is to deeply understand things and their relations to each other. This is where intelligence lies. The fact of being quick or slow isn't really relevant. Naturally, it's helpful to be quick, like it is to have a good memory. But it's neither necessary or sufficient for intellectual success.
>
> (*Schwartz, 2001, pp. 30-31*)

Answering questions in front of others – performance subject

Sometimes maths is presented as being all about performance rather than the process. League tables are displayed ranking learners according to how many questions they got right. Learners are put on the spot to answer questions in front of their peers. This can be extremely distressing for learners who lack confidence in maths. Maths is a subject where there is nowhere to hide. $7 \times 6 = 42$, is a fact. You can't offer your interpretation of it! Far better would be to celebrate individual improvements – for example, a child who has gone from getting two out of ten questions right to three out of ten has improved by 50%. That is something to be celebrated. They should be top of the league table. Making sure that learners have sufficient time to answer and are not put on the spot is an easy win for maths teachers.

Working in isolation

Whilst there is a need to work independently so that progress can be assessed, this should only be a small part of the lesson. Most of the time learners should work collaboratively, supporting each other and sharing their ideas. This has many benefits, including expanding their mathematical vocabulary and developing flexibility in approach. In Singapore, which is known for its success in teaching maths, learners are always grouped in mixed-ability groups, so that the learners who have grasped a particular concept can support those who are struggling with that concept. Maths is a very diverse subject and not all learners will struggle with all aspects of it. There will be some lessons where learners who previously needed support are now the ones providing the support and this can be very beneficial to learners with low self-esteem in maths. Our dyslexic learners often have highly developed visual and spatial skills and are well placed to support seemingly high-achieving children who tend to work at a more abstract level.

MINDSET

There are two types of mindset in maths learning: growth mindset and fixed mindset. Growth mindset refers to a learner's attitude to their maths ability and potential in maths. Learners with a growth mindset believe that they can improve their maths ability. However, learners with a fixed mindset believe that their ability in maths is never going to change, no matter what they do.

This is often perpetuated by parents, who state that they were 'terrible at maths' when they were at school as a way of comforting their child when they do poorly in maths. This promotes a fixed mindset in the child who will then believe that you are born either good or bad at maths and there is nothing you can do about it.

Carol Dweck, in her book *Mindset: How You Can Fulfil Your Potential*, dispels this mathematical myth by exploring the power of our mindset. She explains why it's not just our abilities and talent that bring us success, but whether we have adopted a fixed or growth mindset in our approach. With the right mindset, learners can improve their motivation and attainment.

PARENTS

As mentioned in the previous section, parents can be the cause of maths anxiety. Learners will pick up on negative perceptions of maths from their parents.

It may be that the parents are trying to help but are using a different method and this can be confusing and frustrating for both parties.

SUMMARY

- Maths anxiety is very common.
- If left unidentified, it can have a very detrimental effect on a learner.
- Symptoms and causes are widespread.
- Often it is the way maths is taught that causes the anxiety.

REFERENCES

Jackson, Elizabeth (2008) Mathematics anxiety in student teachers. *Practitioner Research in Higher Education*, 2 (1), pp. 36–42.

Maloney, E. A., Ramirez, G., Gunderson, E. A., Levine, S. C., & Beilock, S. L. (2015) Intergenerational effects of parents' math anxiety on children's math achievement and anxiety. *Psychological Science*, 26(9), pp. 1480–1488. https://doi.org/10.1177/0956797615592630

Richardson, F. C., & Suinn, R. M. (1972). The Mathematics anxiety rating scale: Psychometric data. *Journal of Counseling Psychology*, 19(6), pp. 551–554. https://doi.org/10.1037/h0033456

Schwartz, Laurent-Moïse. (2001). *A Mathematician Grappling with His Century*. Basel, Switzerland: Birkhäuser.

Tobias, S., & Weissbrod, C. (1980). Anxiety and mathematics: An update. *Harvard Educational Review*. 50(1), pp. 63–70. https://doi.org/10.17763/haer.50.1.xw483257j6035084

INDICATORS OF DYSCALCULIA

It can be difficult to distinguish between dyscalculia and general maths learning difficulties. Where does one end and the other begin? General maths difficulties are more likely to be attributed to external factors such as missing a lot of school or having inadequate teaching. Dyscalculia is due to internal factors, a difference in the way that the brain is wired. However, some learners may have both internal and external factors at play, making it even harder to identify whether the learner has dyscalculia or not. Try to look out for unexpected difficulty in maths, maybe a child who is coping well in all other areas but just can't seem to grasp basic maths. Other learners may be OK with some aspects of maths, e.g. shape and space, but find number work and fact recall very challenging.

These are some of the indicators of dyscalculia that you may notice.

1. AN INABILITY TO SUBITISE EVEN VERY SMALL QUANTITIES

The word 'subitise' comes from the Latin word 'subito' which means suddenly. It refers to our ability to immediately recognise the number of items in a set without actually having to count them. Most people can subitise up to five or six randomly arranged items. A dyscalculic learner may not be able to do this and may have difficulty in subitising just three items.

DOI: 10.4324/9781003326625-4

Whilst we can train learners to recognise patterns of dots and to develop their ability to subitise, this can be a lifelong problem for learners with dyscalculia.

Even as adults, it can be difficult to recognise small quantities instantly. For example, on seeing a bowl of fruit containing four apples a dyscalculic adult may still need to count each individual apple rather than instantly recognising that there are four apples in the bowl.

2. POOR NUMBER SENSE

Definitions of number sense vary, but I believe it is our ability to understand our number system and how one number relates to another. A child with good number sense will manipulate numbers and use them flexibly. Learners with poor number sense find it hard to develop meaning for numbers and operations. They don't look for relationships and connections among numbers and operations and they don't have any flexibility in the way that they use numbers.

Number sense is also about decision-making, knowing what strategy will be the most effective and having a range of strategies to choose from.

For example, when multiplying 19 × 18 we may first calculate 20 × 18 and then subtract 18 to give us the answer. This is a more efficient method than doing a long multiplication.

Method 1	Method 2
20 × 18 = 360	19
360 − 18 = 342	× 18
	152
	+ 190
	342

Which method do you prefer?

3. AN INABILITY TO ESTIMATE WHETHER A NUMERICAL ANSWER IS REASONABLE

Being able to estimate an answer is an incredible advantage when doing maths, but learners with dyscalculia find this extremely hard. You can place a set of counters in front of them (say 15) and they may come up with anything from 2 to 200! This also applies to calculations, so when adding 99 and 190, they won't be looking for an answer that is near to 300. They may add 190 and 99 and get 1,999, and not be alerted to the unreasonableness of this answer.

Being unable to estimate stems from magnitude processing difficulties in learners with dyscalculia. They have not developed the ability to associate numerical magnitude to a numerical symbol; 99 and 190 have no meaning in terms of numerical magnitude to these learners. That is why it is so important that we use concrete manipulatives to help these learners to develop an understanding of numerical magnitude. If they can physically see the difference between 99 and 190 through the use of manipulatives such as Dienes blocks then we can help them to develop their estimation skills. Many children are reluctant to estimate an answer as they see it as an unnecessary step and extra work, but developing the ability to estimate is one of the most powerful skills that we can teach learners as it will help them to identify errors that they have made and will help them to keep on the right track in multi-step calculations.

4. IMMATURE STRATEGIES

Dyscalculic learners tend to cling on to procedures that they feel secure with, for example, counting all instead of counting on when adding two numbers. They don't have the confidence to play with the numbers or to try out new, more efficient methods. In this respect they often end up doing a harder, more time-consuming version of maths as they will apply longwinded and inefficient procedures instead of seeing a quicker, more efficient route to the answer.

I have seen children start to draw dots when adding two three-digit numbers together, as this was a strategy that worked for them when adding one-digit numbers together. Clearly this is a very inefficient and immature strategy, but it is typical of learners with dyscalculia who will stick to a procedure that has worked for them in the past.

5. INABILITY TO NOTICE PATTERNS

Being able to see patterns in maths makes it much easier for us to generalise and to predict solutions. Learners with dyscalculia will find this very difficult as they are unable to easily spot the patterns in maths. We cannot assume that a dyscalculic learner will spot a pattern even if it seems obvious to us. For example, when looking at the five times table there is a very clear pattern in the ones digit:

$1 \times 5 = 5$
$2 \times 5 = 10$
$3 \times 5 = 15$
$4 \times 5 = 20$
$5 \times 5 = 25$

It is clear that the next product table fact will end in 0 but this is not obvious to learners with dyscalculia. In the early stages, pattern recognition can be developed through simple AB patterns and then more complex ABC patterns. The first stage is to recognise a pattern and then to be able to continue that pattern before finally being able to generate your own pattern. The activities in early years set foundation for later learning and the importance of developing these skills cannot be underestimated.

6. INABILITY TO GENERALISE

Generalising is all about being able to transfer acquired knowledge to a new situation. The ability to do this helps us to make sense of maths and to understand the connections and patterns.

Dyscalculic learners struggle with generalisation of ideas and concepts and find it hard to transfer information from one area of maths to another. Consequently, for these learners, maths is a multitude of individual pieces of information that have to be stored and remembered or calculated from first principles every time.

7. DELAY IN COUNTING

Dyscalculic learners have a marked delay in counting and understanding the counting principles such as cardinality and one-to-one correspondence. They tend to persist in using immature counting strategies. Counting backward will be a particular difficulty. So it is important to count backwards as often as you count forwards. The counting principles are detailed in Chapter 5 and, again, understanding these principles will be key to any future learning in maths.

8. DIFFICULTY IN RECALLING TABLES AND NUMBER FACTS

Dyscalculic learners have a marked difficulty in remembering arithmetical facts such as times tables and number bonds. This makes is much harder for them to carry out simple calculations, particularly if they have to do them mentally. One of the reasons for this is that they have not attached the numerical magnitude to the numerical symbol. When they see '3' they don't have an image of three items in their mind.

9. DIFFICULTY DECOMPOSING NUMBERS

Dyscalculic learners find it very hard to break numbers up into smaller parts, for example, recognising that 10 is made up of 4 and 6, 7 and 3, 8 and 2, etc. The ability to decompose and recompose numbers can be seen as a precursor to numerical development. Learners without this sense of how numbers are constructed will struggle to develop fluency in mathematical thinking.

SUMMARY

- It can be difficult to identify whether difficulties are caused by internal or external factors, or a combination of the two.
- Dyscalculia is characterised by poor number sense, inability to subitise and difficulty with symbolic and non-symbolic magnitude.

DEBUNKING THE MYTHS

There are many myths around maths and dyscalculia, some of which are widely believed. This section will look at common myths surrounding dyscalculia and explain why they are not true.

MYTH 1: NOT MANY LEARNERS HAVE DYSCALCULIA

This is untrue. Around 5–8% of the population are believed to be dyscalculic. The problem here is that not many learners are identified with dyscalculia. There is a lot more awareness around dyslexia than there is around dyscalculia. In 2018, Queen's University in Belfast carried out a study to ascertain the prevalence of dyscalculia in primary school-age learners. The found that 6% of the 2,400 learners tested had dyscalculia. This equates to 144 learners. Out of the 144 learners with dyscalculia, only one child had been formally identified.

MYTH 2: DYSCALCULIA IS DYSLEXIA WITH NUMBERS

This is a phrase often used as an over-simplification of the term dyscalculia. However, the areas of the brain that are responsible for dyslexia are completely separate from the areas of the brain that are responsible for dyscalculia. Dyslexia is a language-based difficulty associated with phonological awareness deficit. Dyscalculia is number-based and associated with a magnitude processing deficit. It is true, though, that there is a greater co-occurrence of dyslexia and dyscalculia than would be statistically expected, given individual prevalence.

DOI: 10.4324/9781003326625-5

MYTH 3: SOME PEOPLE ARE JUST NOT MATHS PEOPLE

This is probably one of the most common myths. There is the belief that you are just born good or bad at maths. This is simply not true. The brain is incredibly plastic and given the right environment and the right teaching, we can all learn to do maths. We may not all enjoy it as much as other subjects, but that is due to the heterogeneity of humans rather than the subject itself. Promoting a growth mindset in learners will go a long way towards dispelling this myth. Learners with a growth mindset embrace the power of 'yet': 'I cannot do this yet, but that does not mean that I will never be able to do it'.

MYTH 4: YOU CAN'T DIAGNOSE DYSCALCULIA UNTIL KEY STAGE 2

There used to be the idea that you couldn't identify dyslexia until a child was seven years old. This was a travesty as it meant that many learners were suffering years of failure and frustration before any specialist support could be put in place. We now know that early identification is key. The sooner that we recognise that there is an issue, the sooner we can put measures in place to help. The same is true for dyscalculia. Many of the signs of dyscalculia will show up in very early maths concepts. The basic counting principles which learners will grasp by around four or five years old will not be understood by a dyscalculic child. So the signs are there at a very early age. We can look for learners who have not gained cardinality or conservation of number. Do they have 1:1 correspondence? Can they find a set of four objects? Can they say which of two sets has more?

MYTH 5: DYSCALCULIA IS ANOTHER NAME FOR MATHS ANXIETY

Many learners with dyscalculia will have maths anxiety, but there are also many learners who are high achievers in maths who also have maths anxiety. The two things are completely different. Maths anxiety has a wide range of causes and is based on emotional responses to different situations. Dyscalculia is a difference in the way that the brain is wired.

There are some cases where the maths anxiety is so severe that the child presents as though they are dyscalculic. This is sometimes referred to as pseudo-dyscalculia. It is the severe anxiety rather than a brain difference that is the issue.

MYTH 6: PEOPLE WITH DYSCALCULIA WILL NEVER BE ABLE TO DO MATHS

Again, given the right support and learning environment, we can all learn to do maths. We can all learn how to navigate a mathematical world. We may not do maths for pleasure, but there are many advances in technology that can support people with dyscalculia so that they can function numerically as adults.

SUMMARY

- Dyscalculia affects around 6% of the population. That means that in every classroom there with be one or two learners with dyscalculia (and many more with more general maths learning difficulties).
- Dyscalculia is massively under-identified.
- We can identify the tell-tale signs of dyscalculia at a very young age.

Part 2

PRACTICAL
STRATEGIES

THE TYPICAL DEVELOPMENTAL STAGES OF MATHS IN EYFS AND KEY STAGE 1

We cannot underestimate the importance of the early stages of maths development. There is a great deal for a child to learn and many crucial concepts to understand. Learning to count involves much more than just reciting a sequence of numbers.

I often hear practitioners say 'I'm no good at maths, so I am glad that I teach Early Years. I don't think I could cope with Year 6 maths'. Helping learners to conceptualise our number system is demanding and requires a deep understanding of the counting principles. So, far from the idea that the less confident maths teachers should be in Early Years, I think this is where the most confident maths teachers should be. The foundations need to be deep and strong in order for future learning to be secure.

So, what are these counting principles?

COUNTING PRINCIPLES

STABLE ORDER

This is understanding that we always count in the same order: 1, 2, 3, 4, 5, etc. We can't change this order as we have a set number name for each numerical quantity. It is important that learners have the opportunity to count backwards as well as forwards.

DOI: 10.4324/9781003326625-7

ONE-TO-ONE CORRESPONDENCE

This is understanding that each item has one count only. You may have seen learners miscounting their fingers as they are saying the number names quicker than they can touch their fingers. They confidently tell you that they have 6 fingers! This is indicative of the child not having gained the concept of 1:1 correspondence.

CARDINALITY

This is understanding that the last number we say when we count a set is how many items there are in that set. Learners who haven't mastered cardinality will recount their fingers from one each time and have not realised that once they have counted five fingers, they don't need to count from one again.

CONSERVATION OF NUMBER

This is understanding that three items spread far apart on a table is the same numerical quantity as three items close together. Three is three, however it is arranged.

ORDER IRRELEVANCE

This is understanding that when we count a set of objects it doesn't matter which object we choose to start counting from. The total number in the set will be the same, whatever the order we count them in.

MOVEMENT IS MAGNITUDE

This is understanding that as we move up the counting sequence the numbers get bigger by one each time.

ABSTRACTION

This is understanding that three elephants are not numerically more than three mice, just because the elephants are physically larger. It is also understanding that we can count things that we can't touch, like sounds and also that we can represent quantities of real objects such as apples with counters or cubes.

HIERARCHICAL INCLUSION

This is understanding that within a set of numbers are smaller sets. For example, within a set of five items there are sets of one and four, or sets of two and three.

UNITISING

This is being able to count in groups – for example in twos or threes – and leads on to our understanding of our place value system. Once a count exceeds nine then we have one group of ten.

On top of this learners need to go through the different levels of oral counting.

LEVELS OF ORAL COUNTING

STRING LEVEL

At this level, learners can't distinguish one number name from another and counting is a continuous sound string 'onetwo-threefour'. This is very similar to when learners learn the alphabet and say elemenope for 'lmnop' as it if was one letter sound.

UNBREAKABLE LIST LEVEL

At this level, learners can identify distinct number names, but always start counting at one.

BREAKABLE CHAIN LEVEL

At this level, learners can start counting from any number and this is essential if they are going to be able to use counting on as a strategy for addition.

NUMERABLE CHAIN LEVEL

At this level, sequence, count and cardinality are merged so if you are counting from three, then three is the first number, four is the second number, etc....

BI-DIRECTIONAL CHAIN

At this level a child can say the numbers in either direction and start at any point. This is essential for counting back as a strategy for subtraction.

TYPICAL DEVELOPMENT OF MATHS SKILLS FROM AGE THREE TO AGE SEVEN

It is impossible to give an exact age at which these skills will develop as learners will all learn at different rates. I am often asked, 'At what age should a child be able to subitise five items?' and many other similar questions. My rule of thumb is always to look out for the child that hasn't grasped something when the majority of their peers have. Also, be mindful of the child's birth month. Are they one of the youngest in the class or one of the eldest?

Having said that, it is useful to have a guide for typical development and I have set this out below as a rough guide to typical expectations at different ages. This list has been adapted from www.learningtrajectories.org, which is an excellent website offering examples of the different stages of development and activities for supporting learners at each stage.

The NCETM also have useful guidance on typical progression: www.ncetm.org.uk/in-the-classroom/early-years/.

Many schools are also referring to the ready to progress documents: https://assets.publishing.service.gov.uk/government /uploads/system/uploads/attachment_data/file/1017683/ Maths_guidance_KS_1_and_2.pdf.

All these documents will give you an idea of typical progression and clearly understanding this will help you to identify learners that are not following a typical trajectory.

Typical development in maths from age three to seven	
Three years old	Beginning to count out loud but may be inconsistent in the sequence and may miss out numbers. Beginning to develop 1:1 correspondence but inconsistent. Can make small collections of up to three items. Can give the number name for collections of items up to three.
	Can perceptually subitise up to four items. Can compare groups of identical items and identify which group has more or less than the other. Beginning to understand ordinality in terms of 1st and 2nd position.
Four years old	Can count to ten accurately and beginning to count 1:1 but may miss items or count items twice. Beginning to understand cardinality, will accurately count objects in a line and can answer 'how many' by knowing the last number they say in the count is how many there are in the set. Begins to count randomly arranged objects up to ten. Beginning to read and write numerals to ten. Can select groups of objects up to five on demand. Can perceptually subitise up to five items. This means automatic and instant recognition of a set of randomly arranged items.
	Conceptual subitising five, six and seven items. This means that learners are perceptually subitising two smaller groups and combining them to state how many are in the set. For example, seeing a group of three and a group of four in a group of seven and using this to state there are seven in the group. This is the beginning of part-part whole thinking.

Can compare sets of different items and identify that they have the same number in each set. This shows that they are attending to the numerical quantity rather than the difference between the objects.

Learners may still be confused when you have a numerically larger number of smaller items compared to a numerically smaller number of large items.

Beginning to construct a mental number line. For example, when given a number line labelled zero at one end and five at the other end, they can place two with reasonable accuracy.

Can order quantities up to five; for example, can recognise dot patterns and order them or can order towers of cubes.

Uses counting all as a strategy to find the sum of two sets.

Uses counting back to find out how many are left when one or two items are removed.

May begin to use part-part whole thinking to join two sets.

Can use counting on as a strategy. For example, if you have four books and you need six books, how many more do you need? The child will start at four and then count on two to make six in total.

Knows number bonds up to five.

Can share a group of items using the 'one for me, one for you' strategy.

Understand the concept of fair sharing and that odd numbers can't be shared into equal groups.

Five years old	Can count objects accurately for quantities more than ten. Can track which items have been counted and which are still to be counted. Can count objects in different arrangements. Can draw a set number of items. Can count on from a given number up to 20 or 30. Can count accurately backwards from ten.
	Conceptual subitising five, six and seven items. This means that learners are perceptually subitising two smaller groups and combining them to state how many are in the set. For example, seeing a group of three and a group of four in a group of seven and using this to state there are seven in the group. This is the beginning of part-part whole thinking. Extends understanding of ordinality to ten. For example, learners can identify the position of someone finishing a race. Can compare sets up to ten, even when the objects are of different shapes and sizes.
	Can extend their visualisation of a mental number line up to ten. Can order quantities up to ten, with dot cards, towers of cubes etc. Uses part-part whole thinking for addition and subtraction problems. Can find missing number in problems such as $4 + \_\_ = 7$ Can share items by grouping; for example, giving two items at a time until all items are gone. Begins to recognise unit fractions such as ½, ⅓, ¼.

Six years old	Can give the number one more or one less than another number. Can skip count in twos, fives and tens up to 100. Can count to 100 accurately and can make the decade transitions. Knows number bonds for all numbers up to ten and uses knowledge of bonds to ten to work out bonds to 20. Begins to solve start unknown problems, such as __ + 6 = 10. Begins to generalise; for example, uses the fact that 5 + 5 = 10 to find 5 + 6. Knows doubles to 20.
	Understands place value in terms of tens and ones. Can perform two-digit addition with renaming. Begins to understand that multiplication and division are inverse operations. Uses repeated addition for multiplication and grouping for division. Begins to understand fraction notation and that a larger denominator represents a smaller fraction.
Seven years old	Confidently counts to 100 and makes the decade transitions starting from any number. Understands place value in terms of the value of the digit in the tens or ones column. Can count in multiples of ten. Can count beyond 100 and understands place value in hundreds, tens and ones.
	Counts forwards and backwards in tens and ones. Can recognise groups of numbers; e.g., fives, tens and twos to help when finding how many. Uses place value to compare numbers. For example, knows that 53 is more than 49 by looking at the tens digit.

	Uses a mental number line to 100 to round numbers or say whether a number is closer to one multiple of ten or another. Begins to extend this to a mental number line to 1,000. Can estimate the number of items in a set up to around 100 items. Uses decomposition of numbers when adding and subtracting.

I have only set out this typical development up until seven as by that age the crucial building blocks of maths have been introduced. There will be variation in development from child to child but this overview will give you a rough guide as to what to expect at each age. It is important to make sure that we don't move learners on too quickly, despite what the curriculum may dictate! Maths is intrinsically a cumulative subject and if we move on to a new concept before the prerequisite knowledge has been understood then we are storing up a great deal of trouble for the future.

SUMMARY

- The foundations of counting need to be fully understood.
- Spend time on the counting principles.
- Look out for children who are not following the typical learning trajectories and provide intervention as soon as any difficulties arise.

GOOD PRACTICE

Now that the typical stages of development have been detailed, this chapter will explore good practice for supporting learners with dyscalculia and maths learning difficulties. As is always the case, what works well for learners who are struggling will be beneficial for all learners and there are five core competencies that we need to develop in order for learners to gain more than a superficial understanding of maths. These five competencies are the cornerstones of the mastery approach to teaching maths which has proved to be so successful in countries such as Singapore. This approach is being more widely adopted in the United Kingdom and fits very well with the approaches that work for learners with difficulties in maths as it is reliant on developing visualisation, generalisation and number sense. It strengthens the areas of weakness found in learners with dyscalculia and more general maths learning difficulties.

FIVE CORE COMPETENCIES

Whenever we teach maths, it is important that we have these five competencies in mind, both when we are planning a lesson and also when we are assessing a learner's progress. The five competencies are:

- Metacognition.
- Number sense.
- Visualisation.
- Generalisation.
- Communication.

There is no specific hierarchy here, and each competence overlaps with the others. They are all equally important.

DOI: 10.4324/9781003326625-8

METACOGNITION

The Rose review (2009) defined metacognition as 'A term used to describe the understanding of one's own learning processes'.

Another very common phrase used to describe metacognition is 'thinking about your thinking'. In essence, it is an understanding of how you, as an individual, learn best.

WHY IS METACOGNITION SO IMPORTANT?

Understanding how you learn can be very empowering for a struggling learner as well as being very motivating. The learner can select ways of working that they know will be more successful than others, and select methods that are more efficient and effective for them. Often learners with dyscalculia and maths learning difficulties approach maths in a very procedural way. At some point, they will have been shown a method that works and they will apply that method regardless of the situation or whether that method is appropriate.

For example, when presented with the calculation 1001−999, a procedural approach would be to do a column subtraction:

 1001
- 999

This will involve a longwinded and completely unnecessary calculation. A learner with metacognitive awareness will look at the problem and pause to think before attempting to solve it. They will think about different ways of solving the problem and will then select the most appropriate strategy. Teachers can facilitate the development of metacognitive skills by asking questions of the learners and by also encouraging the learners to question themselves. In the 1980s, Schoenfeld conducted an experiment that showed that learners performed better if they asked themselves simple questions such as, 'What am I doing right now?' and 'Why am I doing it?' There are three distinct phases in metacognition and these are to plan, monitor and evaluate.

PLANNING PHASE

We really need to encourage learners with dyscalculia and maths learning difficulties to stop, think and make a plan before they embark on a calculation. I am not going to pretend that this will be easy and it won't come naturally to these learners, but after time, when they realise that this planning stage is making life easier for them, it will become part of their daily approach to maths.

Part of the planning stage is to ask themselves some questions. For example:

- *What is the question asking me to do?*
- *What should I do first?*
- *Have I seen a problem like this before?*
- *What strategies worked for that problem?*
- *Can I apply them here?*
- *Where can I go for help?*
- *Do I need any manipulatives to help me?*
- *Can I draw a diagram?*

It can be useful for learners to be given a list of such questions to remind them to think before they start trying to solve the problem. Once the learners have decided on a plan of action, they can start to solve the problem and move on to the next phase of monitoring.

MONITOR

The learner now needs to monitor their progress. This again entails asking themselves questions such as:

- *Is the plan working?*
- *How am I getting on?*
- *Is this strategy working?*
- *What other methods could I use?*
- *Am I getting nearer to the answer?*

HAVE I SELECTED THE BEST STRATEGY?

Often learners with dyscalculia are reluctant to try new methods. They are even more reluctant to follow their own ideas as they lack the confidence that they will be selecting a suitable method. By encouraging them to monitor in this way, they have the opportunity to change their approach and try out different methods. Later on, they may be able to reflect on which method was the more effective and efficient.

For example, when subtracting 999 from 1,001, they may decide to use a number line rather than column subtraction and count on two from 999 to reach 1,001. They may decide to model 1,001 using base ten and then they may 'see' that 999 is two less than 1,001.

The more we can expose learners to a variety of methods, the greater their repertoire of approaches will be. It does take time and patience, but is worth the effort as it will move the learners away from longwinded, unnecessary procedures to a more efficient reasoning-based approach. This will save them a lot of time and effort in the future.

Once the problem has been solved the learners can move into the evaluate phase.

EVALUATE

The learners now need to reflect on how effective or efficient their approach was. Again, they can ask themselves questions such as:

- *Did I solve the problem?*
- *Did I use the most efficient strategy?*
- *Could I have done anything better?*
- *Was there something that I did not understand?*
- *Could I apply what I have done here to other problems in the future?*

They may want to compare their approach with approaches used by their peers and discuss what they have done. This is a good opportunity for them to try and explain their thinking and to listen to explanations from other learners. This again will boost their mathematical toolbox as well as developing their mathematical language.

HOW CAN WE HELP LEARNERS TO DEVELOP THEIR METACOGNITIVE AWARENESS?

Learners with dyscalculia may be reluctant to question themselves so we can help by prompting them, at each of the three phases.

We can discuss strategies with them, and let them write down their ideas or strategies if they want to. We can ask them to assess their approach once the problem has been solved and evaluate how effective it was. We also need to make sure that we are giving them tasks that lend themselves to multiple approaches.

I have detailed some questions that will help the learners to think even more deeply about how they approach maths and how they can improve.

Questions that help to develop an awareness of how they learn:

- *What did you learn?*
- *What do you believe was the purpose of today's problem?*
- *How did you learn it?*
- *Did you find anything very difficult?*
- *Did you find anything very easy?*
- *How did you do this task?*
- *What equipment did you use to help you?*
- *Did it help to talk about the problem?*
- *Did it help to draw a diagram?*
- *What else could you have done?*

Questions that help to develop an awareness of attitudes and feelings:

- *What did you enjoy about solving that problem?*
- *What was good about the problem?*
- *Was there a part of the problem that you did not enjoy? Why?*
- *Where could you have gone for help?*

Questions that help to develop an awareness of setting goals:

- *Could you have done anything better?*
- *Could you have used a more efficient method?*

- *What would you like to work on next?*
- *What will help you in achieving your next target?*

Developing metacognitive awareness will benefit all learners in the class, but particularly the learners who are struggling. Generally speaking, metacognitive awareness develops around eight years of age, but we can still use these questions with younger learners to help them see that there are often multiple approaches and some are more effective than others. Metacognition depends on the ability to make decisions and this is an important part of number sense.

NUMBER SENSE

Number sense is our ability to be flexible with numbers and to understand how numbers relate to each other.

> It can be thought of as 'good intuition' about numbers and their relationships. It develops gradually as a result of exploring numbers, visualizing them in a variety of contexts, and relating them in ways that are not limited by traditional algorithms.
>
> *(Howden 1989)*

Number sense is:

- An awareness and understanding about what numbers are.
- Their relationships.
- Their magnitude.
- The relative effect of operating on numbers.
- Including the use of mental maths and estimation.

(Fennell and Landis, 1994)

Learners with poor number sense rely on rote learning and applying procedures. The rarely use reasoning and generalising when tackling mathematical tasks. For example, a child with good number sense would see 29 + 30 + 31 as 3 × 30, as this is a quicker way of working out the answer. A child with poor number sense would not see the relationship between these numbers and would probably follow the standard procedure of column addition. Learners who have poor number sense are effectively doing a much harder version of maths. They are in effect doubly disadvantaged as they are struggling with maths and doing a very complicated version of it.

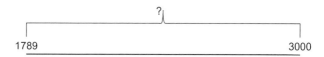

Think about how you would calculate 3,000 - 1,789? What strategies could you use? Is a column subtraction the best option?

Most learners will find the answer using a column subtraction, but we could use our number sense to make this problem much simpler. When we are subtracting one number from another we are finding the difference between the two numbers. In other words, we are looking for the distance between these two numbers if they were placed on a number line.

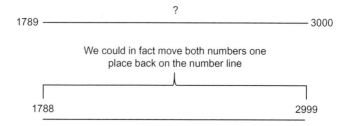

Now the calculation is 2,999 - 1,788 and this is much simpler to perform as a column subtraction. So that one small step, based on our understanding of subtraction, has taken all the difficulty out of the problem.

HOW TO DEVELOP NUMBER SENSE

Number sense develops through playing with numbers and discovering what you can and can't do. Making mistakes and learning from them is all part of the process as is trying out new ideas and methods. There are two important skills that will help a learner to develop number sense, estimation and flexibility.

Magnitude processing and estimation

Estimation is a key skill in maths. Learners with magnitude processing difficulties will struggle with estimation and this will impact on their monitoring of their learning in maths as they won't be alerted to any mistakes that they have made. Learners who struggle with maths are reluctant to develop their estimation skills, not only because they find it difficult, but also because they see it as an extra and unnecessary calculation. However, the more that we can help learners to develop this skill the better developed their number sense will be, and they will be more likely to recognise when they have made a mistake. Estimation skills and appreciation of magnitude can be developed quite early on by comparing piles of counters or cubes.

ACTIVITY

Place two piles of counters or cubes into two identical bowls. It is best if you can use counters or cubes that are all the same colour and size as this will mean that the only variation is in the numerical quantity and the learner won't be distracted by any other variable.

Start off with very few in one bowl and a much larger quantity in the second bowl. Talk to the learner about which bowl has more and which has less.

Now gradually make the difference in quantity between the two bowls less, until each bowl has the same amount. Talk to them about how they could find out which bowl has more. How can they find out if each bowl has the same number of items? Encourage the learner to match items one to one for smaller quantities or to count in groups of five or ten for larger quantities. The discussion of counting strategies that they can choose from is key here.

Once they are more confident in comparing sets, then you can introduce comparing sets of different sized objects. For example, three large balls compared with ten marbles. Which has more? This will help the learner focus on the numerical quantity rather than the physical size.

Once the learner has had experience of comparing sets then you can move on to estimation. This time we will only have one set of items, but again they should be identical. Start with no more than 20 objects and ask the learner if they can guess how many there are. If their guess is wildly out, then ask them to count out two or three shapes. Ask them to look at the amount of space the objects take up. Then ask them if they can now make a revised estimation, based on the space that three shapes took up. Once they are making reasonable estimates you can move on to larger quantities and introduce counting in groups of five or ten to help them when checking their estimations.

Another important skill is to be able to work with number lines: to visualise number lines and to place numbers correctly on blank number lines. This will help the learner to appreciate how one number relates to another and also to develop their sense of magnitude. In early years when placing numbers on a number line, learners will often bunch up the numbers to the left-hand side and won't space them evenly. They may do something like this:

0   1 2 3 4 5   6   7   8 9 10

To help understand the numerical value of numbers 0–10 and how they relate to one another, we can use five and ten frames.

FIVE FRAMES

A five frame is simply a grid with five squares. Numbers can be represented by placing counters or cubes in the grid.

TEN FRAMES

Ten frames are 2×5 grids used to represent the numbers 0-10.

ACTIVITY

To help learners to develop their understanding of numerical magnitude we can ask them to place counters on the frame

Start by giving the learner three counters and ask them to place them on a five frame.

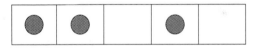

Explore different ways of placing the counters. Ask the learner what each arrangement tells them about the number three.

By discussing the arrangements, the learner will discover conservation of 3 (3 is 3 however it is arranged) and also the way that 3 is made up, for example 1 + 1 + 1 or 2 + 1. Each arrangement also shows us that 3 is less than 5 and is always 2 less than 5 as there are 2 spaces. This helps them to understand the magnitude of 3 in comparison to 5.

Now give the learner a number line, either using a white board or piece of paper, with 0, 5 and 10 marked and ask them to try and place 3 on the number line. They should have a better appreciation of where 3 'lives' in comparison to 5. If they still struggle with this then repeat the work on five and ten frames and use number tracks instead of number lines, as below. Number tracks are easier to work with than number lines as they are a discrete representation rather than a continuous one. On a number track, the number after 3 is 4 and there is nothing in between. On a number line, there are an infinite number of numbers between 3 and 4 (3.002, 3.5672, etc.).

0					5					10

Repeat this process for numbers up to five and then introduce a ten frame for numbers up to ten.

ROUNDING

Another important skill when estimating is the ability to round numbers. Rather than just relying on learning that five or more rounds up and less than five rounds down you can use a diagram to help. This visualisation can really help learners when rounding numbers. This diagram has been used by Steve Chinn.

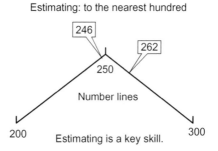

Estimating: to the nearest hundred

The zig zag lines are labelled in multiples of 50 (or whatever is appropriate for the size of number you are working with). The number to be rounded is then placed on the zig zag according to its size and followed down the slope to give the number that it rounds to.

Being able to round will help learners develop a sense of reasonableness when looking at the answer to a calculation. Is the answer anywhere near their estimation? Learners with magnitude processing and estimation difficulties will find it hard to round at an appropriate degree of accuracy. They tend to be too accurate. For example, when adding 1,089 to 8,012 they may round to the nearest 10 instead of the nearest 1,000. The more that we can practice rounding and estimating the better their sense of reasonableness will be.

Flexibility

A person with good number sense will be flexible in the way that they work with numbers. They will have a range of approaches and strategies in their mathematical toolbox and will select the most efficient approach or they will adjust the numbers to make the calculation easier. We saw earlier how much easier it is to subtract 1,788 from 2,999 than it is to subtract 1,789 from 3,000. It is this flexibility that enables learners with good number sense to access this easier version of maths.

Understanding how numbers can be broken into parts and how they can be combined will give us flexibility and options when we are calculating. An understanding of the four operations is key here as well. For example, knowing that addition and subtraction are inverse operations or that addition and multiplication are commutative but subtraction and division are not. It is all about knowing what we can and can't do with numbers, and vitally when to do it!

VISUALISATION

Visualisation is our ability to have a mental image of the maths that we are doing. Albert Einstein famously said, 'If I can't see it then I can't understand it'.

The Open University states

> Imagery is a powerful force for perception and understanding. Being able to 'see' something mentally is a common metaphor for understanding it. An image may be of some geometrical shape, or of a graph or diagram, or it may be some set of symbols or some procedure.

Visualisation is very much the pictorial element of the concrete, pictorial, abstract approach to teaching maths. It is the bridge that joins the concrete and abstract representations and without it learners will either be stuck at the concrete stage or will have moved to the abstract stage too quickly without any depth of understanding.

Jerome Bruner proposed the concrete, pictorial, abstract (CPA) approach in 1966. He believed that the abstract nature of maths is a 'mystery' to many learners, so needs to be scaffolded with concrete and pictorial representations of the maths.

As an example of the importance of visualisation let's create a sequence by adding up consecutive odd numbers:

1
1 + 3
1 + 3 + 5
1 + 3 + 5 + 7

And so on.

This generates the following sequence.

1 4 9 16 25 36 49

Do those numbers look familiar? They are, of course, the square numbers.

Now, that in itself is all well and good, but why is that happening? Why does the sum of consecutive odd numbers create square numbers?

It is hard to understand and even harder to explain without the use of a diagram. But once we have a diagram, once we can 'see' the problem then it all makes perfect sense.

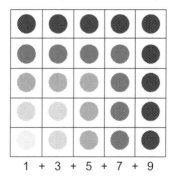

1 + 3 + 5 + 7 + 9

It also begs the question what happens if I create a similar sequence using even numbers? There are two questions that I would always ask in a maths lesson.

What do you notice?

What do you wonder?

In this example, we notice that adding consecutive odd numbers produces the sequence of square numbers. What we wonder is why and also what happens when we add consecutive even numbers. The 'what do you notice' question encourages children to look for patterns and connections and to explore what is in front of them. The 'what do you wonder' question encourages them to think outside of the box and to generalise their understanding.

If you only ever ask two questions in a maths lesson, those would be the ones to choose.

HOW TO TEACH VISUALISATION

The ability to visualise starts to develop through play before learners even reach school age. Playing with concrete materials such as building blocks is an integral part of the development of visualisation. Ramful and Lowrie (2015) found that boys have better visualisation skills than girls, largely due to the time they spend with construction equipment. All learners use texture and touch to connect to the brain. We can mediate the development of visualisation by asking questions such as:

Can you imagine?

Can you picture?

Can you see the dot pattern of five in the dot pattern of ten?

By giving learners a wide variety of manipulatives, they can use these to model the maths and develop their visualisation skills. Examples of particularly useful manipulatives are:

Ten frames, two-coloured counters, Dienes blocks, Cuisenaire rods. The use of these will be explored in the next two chapters of this book.

We also need to remember that fingers are a great way to represent numbers. The fact that we use a base ten system is rooted in the fact that we have ten fingers!

Berteletti and Booth (2015) studied the somatosensory finger area in the brain, which is used for the perception and representation of fingers. This area lights up when we do maths even if we are not using our fingers. Further research has found finger representation to be a predictor of future maths ability, so the more that learners can develop their finger representation the better placed they will be to visualise maths later on.

Finger representation can be developed by nursery rhymes, that involve counting on your fingers, such as Tommy Thumb and Two Little Dickie Birds.

You can also have more targeted activities, such as asking learners to use their fingers to make bunny ears.

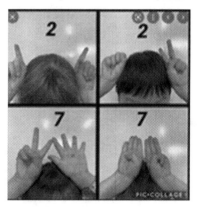

And then ask them to represent different numbers with their fingers.

For example, can they show you 6 by using bunny ears? How many different ways can you do this?

The fact that they can't see their fingers is how this activity can develop visualisation.

GENERALISATION

A lesson without the opportunity for learners to generalise is not a maths lesson.

(*J Mason 1996, p. 65*)

Generalising is all about looking for patterns and connections and then using those patterns and connections to find a general rule. This enables a learner to use what they know to find out something that they don't yet know, such as using the fact that $3 + 4 = 7$ to work out $7,000 - 4,000$.

It is about being able to transfer acquired knowledge to a novel situation. The ability to do this helps us to make sense of maths and to understand the connections and patterns. Dyscalculic learners struggle with generalisation of ideas and concepts and find it hard to transfer information from one area of maths to another. Consequently, for these learners, maths is a multitude of individual pieces of information that have to be stored and remembered or calculated from first principles every time. This places a huge burden on their working memory and it is very difficult for them to store all that information in their long-term memory. This is why a lot of learners with dyscalculia will learn something one day and forget it the next. This can be very frustrating for both teacher and learner as it seems as though little to no progress is being made.

COMMUNICATION

Being able to communicate mathematically is vital if children are going to make good progress. This communication can be in diagrams, orally or in writing.

How many times have you asked a child to explain their mathematical thinking behind an answer they have just given you, only for them to reply 'I just know!'? Learners who respond this way are showing you that their understanding is superficial, and they are unable to explain their thought processes in any depth. This is often a consequence of being taught in a procedural way. It is much easier to just teach a procedure than it is to teach all three components of a mathematical idea however if we only teach the procedure they will only ever have a superficial understanding of that idea.

THREE COMPONENTS OF A MATHEMATICAL IDEA

There are three components of a mathematical idea and each one needs to have equal emphasis when we are teaching maths.

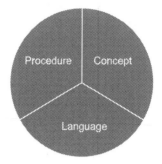

Language component

The language component is the vocabulary and language that we use to communicate a mathematical idea. Professor Mahesh Sharma refers to 'language containers' for concepts that make it easier for a learner to retain their understanding of that concept. For example, the language of multiplication includes the terms product, factor, multiplier and multiplicand. The concept of multiplication is intrinsically linked with division as they are inverse operations. Repeated addition, array and area models are all ways of representing multiplication and in turn can be used to support understanding of division. Being able to describe a mathematical concept using the correct vocabulary enables a learner to communicate their understanding accurately and will help both learners and teacher to ascertain the level of understanding acquired.

Generally speaking, if a learner is struggling with a mathematical idea, then they will also struggle with communicating that idea. Dyscalculic learners may have poor numerosity, but often their linguistic ability is fine. By developing the linguistic component, we are playing to their areas of strength to support their areas of weakness.

Maths word walls should be in every maths classroom, with each new word being added when it is introduced. In this way, learners will build up their repertoire of mathematical terminology and if they are encouraged to verbalise their thinking and to devise their own word problems they will have practice and experience in using this vocabulary correctly.

Conceptual component

This refers to the mathematical idea itself, and is defined by the procedures and language associated with it. For example, when combining two groups together we are demonstrating the concept of addition. We are joining two parts to make one whole. Initially we will model this with concrete manipulatives and then use pictorial representations before moving onto the abstract, symbolic representation. Early maths concepts, such as addition, need to be explored in depth and can't be rushed. They are the bedrock for all future maths and we need to make sure that the foundations are strong before developing more sophisticated concepts.

Procedural component

This is often the most favoured component in a many teaching approaches. It is the 'how' rather than the 'why'. If we just teach the procedure then the learner won't have the full picture of that mathematical idea. If they forget the procedure, then they have nowhere to go to reconstruct that procedure.

Sharma proposes that procedures should be taught through instruction materials that are effective, efficient (not counting) and elegant (can be generalised).

THE IMPORTANCE OF QUESTIONING

Have a bank of questions that are used regularly by all teachers. I often advise schools to decide on a bank of questions that all teachers will ask in a maths lesson across all year groups. This leads to consistency of questioning and language. If learners are constantly being asked these questions they will, eventually, internalise these questions and it will become a natural part of their thinking process. The questions are designed to encourage deeper thinking and understanding and to move learners away from the counting trap and procedural thinking. I have listed some of my favourite questions, but each school setting will want to come up with their own bank of questions.

Example questions

Are you sure?
How do you know?
Are there any other ways?
Does this connect to anything else?
Can you see a pattern?
Can you come up with your own problem?
Can you spot the mistake?
What if ... ?
Is this always true or only sometimes true?
Have you found all the solutions?
Can you set some homework for your parents?
Can you prove it?
Can you draw it?
What resources would help you to solve this problem?
Can you simplify it?
Can you explain it to a friend?

If you have in mind the five core competences every time that you teach maths, then you will be developing learners who think mathematically rather than learners who can follow a procedure. You will also be supporting any learners in your class who are struggling with maths. If the framework of your teaching is embedded with questions that are designed to develop these five core competences then you will be providing them with a very strong and supportive learning environment.

The most effective way to develop the five core competencies and to provide a supportive learning environment is through the use of appropriate manipulatives.

MANIPULATIVES

Manipulative materials are any objects that pupils can touch, move or arrange to model a mathematical idea or concept. They are objects to think with and help learners to explore the patterns and relationships in maths in a concrete way. All learners need to have experience with a wide variety of manipulatives, to develop deeper understanding and also because some manipulatives model a particular concept better than others.

However, many practitioners are unclear as to how to get the most out of the manipulatives they have in their classrooms and many learners simply use them as a crutch or tool to support a particular mathematical procedure. Ofsted's report 'Mathematics: made to measure' suggests that although manipulatives are used in some primary schools to support teaching and learning they are not used as effectively or as widely as they might be. This means that learners are not getting the depth of understanding that they could be achieving through a more consistent and effective use of manipulatives.

> Manipulatives can be important tools in helping students to think and reason in more meaningful ways. By giving students concrete ways to compare and operate on quantities, such manipulatives as pattern blocks, tiles and cubes can contribute to the development of well-grounded, interconnected understandings of mathematical ideas.
>
> *(Stein & Bovalino, 2001)*

One key point is to make sure that your pupils have a wide variety of manipulatives available, for as long as they need them. Using manipulatives over long periods of time is much more beneficial than occasional short-term use. Learners who habitually use manipulatives often can make gains in the following skills:

- Using mathematical language to explain their thinking.
- Relating real-world situations to abstract maths.

- Working collaboratively.
- Thinking more flexibly to find different ways to solve problems.
- Developing metacognition.
- Working independently.
- Being more resilient and persevering with problems.

One particular problem that learners often experience when learning maths is that they see each area of maths as separate and unconnected.

For example, division can be taught as repeated subtraction but learners may also come across fractions in terms of shading segments of a cake and they are unable to make the link between the two concepts. This compartmentalising of maths can be very detrimental to students who are struggling and may have poor number sense. One way to overcome this is to highlight patterns and connections between the different areas of maths by using continuous manipulatives such as base-10 materials (Diene's blocks) and Cuisenaire Rods. Initially learners may prefer to work with discrete materials such as counters, beads or cubes, but it is a good idea to move on from these materials so that they can progress from counting in ones. Using a variety of manipulatives will help learners to make links between areas of maths and see each area as interconnected rather than a compartmentalised subject. The use of manipulatives helps to support learners who are struggling as well as extending more able learners and works for a more inclusive classroom environment and can reduce maths anxiety. Above all, maths is much more fun for students if they have a variety of manipulatives at their fingertips.

HOW CAN WE BEST USE MANIPULATIVES IN THE CLASSROOM?

Common pitfalls

- Learners using manipulatives as crutches to follow a rote procedure rather than as a means to developing understanding.

- Teachers selecting a certain type of manipulative to teach a particular concept.
- Using manipulatives as an add on to a lesson or as a reward.
- Using manipulatives only for learners who are struggling.
- One of the greatest causes of maths anxiety in the classroom comes from manipulatives being taken away too soon, leading to maths becoming abstract and meaningless.

Guidelines for using manipulatives

- Allow free play, let learners discover the properties of the manipulative for themselves.
- Provide access to a wide variety of manipulatives, with learners being able to choose what they want to work with.
- Make manipulatives readily available from Foundation Stage to Key Stage 3 and beyond if required.
- Encourage learners to demonstrate a specific idea using their chosen manipulative.
- Encourage learners to generalise, by demonstrating one concept with a variety of manipulatives.
- Ask learners to show you and each other different ways of solving a problem using a variety of materials.
- The manipulatives need to reinforce the objectives of the lesson.
- The manipulatives must correctly portray the actual maths process or concept.
- Provide explicit instruction on how to use manipulatives.
- Gradually phase out their use as understanding develops.
- Make sure the learners are using the manipulatives to develop understanding.
- Associate the concrete with the pictorial.

By focussing on the five core competencies and using a range of manipulatives we are creating a dyscalculia-friendly classroom which will benefit all learners in the class. There are other ways that you can support learners with dyscalculia and these are detailed below.

CREATING A DYSCALCULIA-FRIENDLY CLASSROOM

It is often said that it is the way maths is taught rather than the subject itself that is the problem for many learners. We can remove many of the barriers to learning by creating a dyscalculia-friendly environment. This will benefit all children, not just those who are struggling with maths.

Here are a few suggestions to help create a dyscalculia friendly environment.

- Use manipulatives as part of your daily routine in maths lessons. Have a wide range of manipulatives, so that the learners can model the problem, using the most effective manipulative for the task in hand. This will also help to develop their visualisation skills. Make sure that manipulatives are available to all learners at all times, thus removing any stigma attached to using them.
- Encourage the children to follow the concrete, pictorial, abstract (CPA) approach. Often, we go straight from the concrete to the abstract and bypass the pictorial altogether, but we really need to make sure that the children are modelling the maths in a concrete way and then representing it pictorially before they move on to the more symbolic abstract representation. If they can visualise the maths then they will be able to draw on that when they are working without any manipulatives.
- Use dot patterns to develop a sense of number. It is best to stick to one pattern to begin with until the learner is confident with recognising the dot patterns for numbers 1-10. Then you can move on to representing numbers with different patterns, encouraging generalisation. You can look at the similarities between dice patterns and dominoes, or you can compare dot patterns to the Numicon tiles. Encourage the leaner to look for patterns within patterns, For example, can they 'see' the dice pattern of three in the dice pattern of five.
- Make your lessons based on games and activities as much as possible, rather than on worksheets. The more actively

involved a learner can be then the more likely they are to retain that knowledge and understanding. Games and activities also help to reduce maths anxiety.

- Make sure that you count backwards with the learners as often as you count forwards and don't always start counting from one. Once a learner is confident in the number system from 1–10 then you can start making connections with scaling by powers of ten. For example, linking 1–10 to 10–100 and 100–1,000. If the learner can see the connections then they are less likely to be afraid of larger numbers.
- Don't assume anything! It is easy to make an assumption that a Year 6 child will have a good grasp of place value, or that they know their two times tables, but we can't assume this is the case just by merit of their year group. Break problems down into small steps and make sure that each step is understood before moving on. This may mean a lot of repetition, consolidation and overlearning.
- Encourage use of the correct mathematical vocabulary and use a range of terms. For example, use a wide variety of ways of expressing 'add'. This will help the learner to understand the concept when presented in different ways. Support the learner in communicating their understanding verbally and in writing as well as by using diagrams.
- Give the learner time to process and understand new information and don't be in a hurry to get to the abstract level of thinking.
- Ask the learners to explain their reasoning, to you and to each other. This can help them to develop their conceptual understanding as well as developing their understanding of mathematical language.
- Make sure that the learners have the prerequisite knowledge needed to develop the new concept; www.learningtra jectories.com is a great website for exploring typical trajectories in mathematical development.
- Encourage the learners to approach problems in a more interactive way. Are there parts that they do understand? What parts don't they understand? Where can they go for support? Promote the idea of questioning what they are

doing at each step rather than just automatically following a procedure without thinking whether that is the best
approach.

- Teach for understanding. Try to avoid rote learning of number
  facts. Teach learners how to use key facts, such as the two
  times, five times and ten times tables, to derive new facts.
- Allow the use of squared paper if the learners have trouble
  setting out their calculations.
- Provide multiplication squares, addition squares and
  100 squares to reduce the load on their working memory.
- Encourage the learners to work in small groups to solve a
  problem rather than in isolation.
- Frequently check in with the learners to ascertain level of
  understanding
- Use low-threshold, high-ceiling tasks. https://nrich.maths
  .org/8769.

These tasks are designed so that they are easy to access but
can be explored at greater depth. This can alleviate maths anxiety as the child who may perceive themselves as struggling
with maths sees that they are doing the same problem as other
learners that they may perceive as being very able in maths.

- Allow the use of calculators for problems that are not purely
  assessing mental maths.

There is a calculator app for people with dyscalculia: https://
apps.apple.com/gb/app/dyscalculator/id508012847.

- Use aperture cards so that the learners can focus on one
  question at a time.

An aperture card is simply a piece of card with a window cut
out so that only one word, problem or question can be viewed
at a time.

- Encourage the learners to make connections from one fact/
  concept to another.

For example, if you know that 6 + 4 = 10, then what else do you know? 60 + 40 = 100? 5 + 5 = 10?, etc.

- Get the learners to create their own word problems.

For example, if 24 is the answer what could the questions be? Write a word problem with 24 as the answer. Or, write an addition word problem using the numbers 5 and 6.

- Give praise for the process rather than the outcome. Removing the emphasis on getting the right answer can really help to alleviate anxiety. The more that we can focus on the strategy and whether the chosen method is helpful, the less anxiety there will be about performance in maths.
- Avoid league tables in class and make sure that you only compare progress against the child's own results.
- Celebrate mistakes and see them as a positive learning opportunity rather than a failure. Having a display of the 'mistake of the week' can make mistakes part of life, part of maths lessons, and something to be explored and learned from rather than something you have done wrong.

SUMMARY

- Every lesson should include open ended questions.
- These questions should develop the five core competencies.

  Metacognition.
  Number sense.
  Visualisation.
  Generalisation.
  Communication.

- Provide a range of manipulatives for all learners in all lessons.
- Provide an environment that is dyscalculia friendly.

REFERENCES

Berteletti I, Booth JR. (2015) Perceiving fingers in single-digit arithmetic problems. *Front Psychol.* Mar 16; 6: 226. doi: 10.3389/fpsyg.2015.00226

Fennell, F., & Landis, T.E. (1994). Number sense and operations sense. In C. A. Thornton & N. S. Bley (Eds.), *Windows of Opportunity: Mathematics for Students with Special Needs* (pp. 187-203). Reston, VA: NCTM.

Howden, H. (1989). Teaching number sense. *The Arithmetic Teacher* 36(6), 6-11. https://doi.org/10.5951/AT.36.6.0006

Mason, J. (1996). Expressing generality and roots of algebra. In N. Bednarz, C. Kieran, & L. Lee (Eds.), *Approaches to Algebra: Perspectives for Research and Teaching* (pp. 65-86). Dordrecht: Kluwe.

Ramful, A., & Lowrie, T. (2015). Spatial visualisation and cognitive style: How do gender differences play out? In M. Marshman, V. Geiger, & A. Bennison (Eds.), *Mathematics Education in the Margins (Proceedings of the 38th Annual Conference of the Mathematics Education Research Group of Australasia)* (pp. 508-515). Mathematics Education Research Group of Australasia. https://core.ac.uk/download/pdf/30343425.pdf

Rose, Jim, Department for Children, Schools and Families (DCSF), corp creator. (2009). Identifying and teaching children and young people with dyslexia and literacy difficulties: An independent report.

Stein, M. K. & Bovalino, J. W. (2001). Reflections on pract ice: Manipulatives: One piece of the puzzle. *Mathematics Teaching in the Middle School* 6(6): 356-360.

7

SPECIFIC STRATEGIES FOR EARLY YEARS AND KEY STAGE 1

Now that we have looked at general good practice we can start to focus on specific strategies to Key Stage 1 and, in Chapter 8, Key Stage 2.

In Chapter 5 we looked at the typical stages of development in maths. This chapter explores specific strategies to help learners reach these developmental stages.

EARLY YEARS

SORTING AND MATCHING

In order to be able to spot patterns and to generalise learners will need extensive early experience of matching and sorting. They need to be able to identify what is the same and what is different when comparing two objects. Initially we can ask learners to sort a collection of objects according to a specific criterion, such as size or shape. Initially we want to make sure that the items are similar in every respect apart from the sorting criteria.

For example:

By only varying one criterion, the learners will have to attend to the only thing that varies, in this case the size of the triangles.

Once they are confident in sorting in this way then we can have two variables and the learners can sort the sets according to different criteria.

For example:

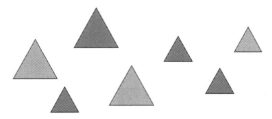

Now the learners can sort by either colour or size. We can then start to encourage the learners to sort and match objects by orientation or function.

For example, all the upside-down teddies in one group and all the right way up teddies in another. For matching by function, we can look at matching a bat with a ball, an egg with an eggcup, etc.

I can't overemphasise how important this experience of sorting and matching is. It is the very foundation of mathematics. What is the same? What is different? is a theme that runs through maths at all ages and stages.

COUNTING

When we learn to count we need to develop a mental image and appreciation of numerical quantity and then match that to the symbol for that quantity. The areas of the brain responsible for this understanding are separate so we need to make the link in our brains between quantity and symbol.

The most important ideas here are the concrete pictorial abstract (CPA) progression and the use of appropriate manipulatives. In the 1960s Bruner put forward the idea that learners need to go through three stages – concrete, pictorial and abstract – in order to fully understand a mathematical concept. Briefly, his model can be described like this:

Concrete. At the concrete level manipulatives are used to explore and solve problems.

Pictorial. At the pictorial level pictures, drawings, diagrams, charts and graphs are used as visual representations of the concrete manipulatives.

Abstract. At the abstract level symbolic representations are used to represent and solve the problem. This is the basis for some of the most successful methods of teaching maths, including the Singapore approach and the approach used by researchers, such as Professor Sharma, in supporting learners with dyscalculia. Without concrete and pictorial experience of a mathematical concept then learners will be working at an abstract level only, which is inaccessible to learners with dyscalculia and also a very superficial and fragile level of understanding.

Even with the CPA progression itself there is a subset within the concrete phase. We refer to this as concrete concrete, concrete pictorial and concrete abstract.

When we start to teach learners to count it is best if we use real objects. For example, real apples, all as similar as possible to each other. This is the concrete concrete stage, as we are using real objects.

Following on from that we can move to concrete pictorial where we are representing quantities with pictures of apples. These can be on card so that the learner can pick them up, thus making them concrete pictorial. After this the learner can move on to the concrete abstract phase. Here the learner will have a concrete object that does not resemble an apple, for example a cube or a counter. I would try to make the concrete object the same colour as the original object so the learner can focus on the progression from the representation of an apple as a picture of an apple to an abstract object we are using to represent the apple.

When information is presented in a book it is naturally a pictorial representation nevertheless we can still go through the pictorial to abstract progression as shown in the following diagrams.

This diagram represents the numbers from 0 to 10 using pictures of apples that are the same colour as an apple.

	0	Zero
🍎	1	One
🍎🍎	2	Two
🍎🍎🍎	3	Three
🍎🍎🍎🍎	4	Four
🍎🍎🍎🍎🍎	5	Five
🍎🍎🍎🍎🍎🍎	6	Six
🍎🍎🍎🍎🍎🍎🍎	7	Seven
🍎🍎🍎🍎🍎🍎🍎🍎	8	Eight
🍎🍎🍎🍎🍎🍎🍎🍎🍎	9	Nine
🍎🍎🍎🍎🍎🍎🍎🍎🍎🍎	10	Ten

Now we can represent the numbers 0 to 10 using an abstract representation of an apple, but still the same colour.

	0	Zero
▨	1	One
▨▨	2	Two
▨▨▨	3	Three
▨▨▨▨	4	Four
▨▨▨▨▨	5	Five
▨▨▨▨▨▨	6	Six
▨▨▨▨▨▨▨	7	Seven
▨▨▨▨▨▨▨▨	8	Eight
▨▨▨▨▨▨▨▨▨	9	Nine
▨▨▨▨▨▨▨▨▨▨	10	Ten

Moving on from this we can use the same abstract representation but vary the visualisation of the number if we want to introduce 10 frames.

	0	Zero
	1	One
	2	Two
	3	Three
	4	Four
	5	Five
	6	Six
	7	Seven
	8	Eight
	9	Nine
	10	Ten

For learners with dyscalculia they may need to go carefully and repeatedly through this progression. If the first representation they are presented with is a picture in a book then they have missed out on several stages that may have been vital to their understanding of the concept.

In Chapter 5 we looked at the skills that learners need to acquire in order to be able to count fluently and to understand our number system. Again, this is something that can't be rushed and it can be hard for practitioners to appreciate how complex learning to count is, as we do it automatically without any thought or effort at all.

One activity that can be particularly useful here is to get the learners to make collections of items. Learners should be counting incidentally as part of daily life, when singing nursery rhymes or counting stairs as they go up and down. They should also be counting sets to find out how many; for example, how many teddies are at the picnic, how many apples in the bowl? The idea here is to make this natural counting a little more directed and focused. Learners can work in pairs to share their counting of different collection of objects and will have the experience of planning, counting and recording. Once all the pairs of learners have completed their collection then strategies can be shared and teachers may decide to model specific strategies.

In terms of resourcing, you will need containers for the objects, such as boxes, bowls or jars. Each should be labelled with the number of items in the container. Make sure that you have an empty container for zero. You may want to label 1–5 in one colour and 6–10 in another colour, especially if you are using five and ten frames to support the counting. Or you may want to have all the even numbers one colour and the odd numbers a different colour. It depends what aspect of our counting system you are trying to emphasise.

The objects in the containers can be identical to begin with, but then you will need to vary the items by one criterion at a time until you have a container of completely different objects. This will help the learners to move on from the principles of 1:1 correspondence and cardinality to abstraction. The items in the containers can be anything that is readily available inside and outside of the classroom, but it is best to avoid items that will distract, such as cars, Lego or balls.

The learners will need equipment to help them count. This may be in the form of five and ten frames to place objects on, or just bowls or cups to place items into 1:1. You can provide number cards and number names so that the learners can label the items they have counted and check that with the original container.

The pairs of learners can now select a container and plan how they are going to count. They may decide to select ten frames or ice cube trays, or they may count in turn. It is entirely up to them to explore different ways of counting and decide on what is the most effective way.

You can support the development of the counting principles by questioning.

- How do you know that you have counted every item?
- Have you counted each item once only? How do you know?
- Does it matter with which item you start counting?
- Do you always have to start your counting with 1? Why?
- Can you count in 2s or 5s (for when the sets are larger)?
- Can you estimate how many items there are?

Now the learners need to decide how they are going to record their counting. They may draw a picture of the objects counted or they may use marks to represent each item. It is important that they are able to decide for themselves how they want to record and then they can compare their ideas with their peers.

DOT PATTERNS

Following on from counting collections of objects, learners can now focus on how numbers can be represented. This can help to develop their understanding of number as well as developing counting principles such as cardinality, 1:1 correspondence and conservation of number.

Number patterns

There are many different arrangements of dots that we can use to represent numbers. Each arrangement tells us something different about our number system. To begin with it doesn't really matter what arrangement you choose to work with as long as you are consistent in using that arrangement until the learner has understood our number system and can recognise the arrangements from 0 to 10. Once they are confident in recognising quantity to 10 then we can start to introduce different representations to generalise their understanding. Here are some examples of the different dot patterns that are commonly used.

Dorean Yeo pattern

Dorean Yeo worked at Emerson house in London, and developed this pattern for the numbers 1 to 10. This pattern focuses on doubles and near doubles. For example, 7 is represented as a 3 and a 4, which is a near double for 8 (which is double 4). Learners are encouraged to look for numbers within numbers and this can help to develop their part/whole thinking.

Number Patterns Dorean Yeo

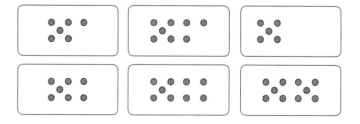

Steve Chinn patterns

Steve's pattern focuses on making 5 and 5 more to give 10. This pattern fits well with the fingers on each hand and also with the use of five and ten frames.

Ten frames

There are two standard ways of filling a ten frame: five wise and pairs wise.

Five wise means that you fill the top row first before moving on to the bottom row. Here we have 5 represented 'five wise':

●	●	●	●	●

Pairs wise means that you fill up the frame column by column from left to right. Here we have 5 represented pairs wise:

●	●	●		
●	●			

Numicon

Numicon is a commercially available product that is commonly used in primary schools. You can see here that Numicon is essentially a pairs wise representation of the numbers 0 to 10.

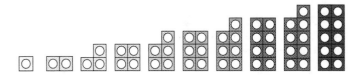

Dominoes

Dominoes give a different representation of number again and are particularly useful if you are working with doubles. They are also useful for generalising representation of a particular number as there are multiple ways of showing numerical quantities.

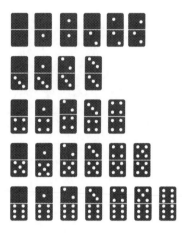

MOVING FROM COUNTING TO PART/WHOLE THINKING

When combining two sets of items learners will initially 'count all', then they move on to the 'counting on' strategy. They may see that there are five items in the first set, by subitising and then count on the items in the second set to find the total. The next stage of development from this is part/whole thinking. In order to develop part/whole thinking, learners need to move from perceptual subitising to conceptual subitising.

Perceptual subitising is instant recognition of a numerical quantity without having to count. Typically, we can instantly recognise up to five items, without counting them.

Conceptual subitising is where we are perceptually recognising two or three smaller amounts of items and then adding them together to make a whole.

Before moving on to conceptual subitising make sure that your learner can perceptually subitise, by doing the following activity.

PERCEPTUAL SUBITISING

Show the learner images of dot patterns or other representations of numbers. Keep the numbers below five. Ask them to immediately say the number that is being represented. Avoid using the word count. When you show the image ask the learners how many dots/lines/fingers, etc. that they can see.

It is important to make sure that you only show the image for about one second. Any longer than that, then the learners will have the opportunity to count.

Use a variety of representations of the same number. The learner needs to appreciate the numerical quantity rather than the way that it is represented. Having multiple representations will help the learner to generalise and make connections.

Pairs game

To vary practising perceptual subitising you can play a pairs game. Make two sets of eight cards. The first set can have numbers represented using ten frames and the second can have numbers represented with fingers. (You can choose whatever representations you wish the learners to work with. The important thing is that you have eight (or more) matching pairs.) Shuffle the cards and place them face down in a four-by-four grid. Players should turn the cards over two at a time. If there is a matching pair those cards are given to the player and the next player takes their turn. If they don't match, then the cards are replaced face down in their original place. The winner is the player with the most pairs. This is also a great game for developing visual memory. Once the learners have had enough experience with a wide range of representations up to five you can move on to conceptual subitising.

CONCEPTUAL SUBITISING

For numbers larger than five, learners will be moving from perceptual subitising to conceptual subitising. The distinction here is that perceptual subitising is instant recognition of quantities up to five and conceptual subitising relies on the recognition of two smaller sets and combining those to be able to recognise quantities of six or more. Conceptual subitising is the basis of part/whole thinking and moves the learner away from counting strategies.

Start with images that are more instantly recognizable and have a set pattern. For example:

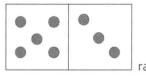 rather than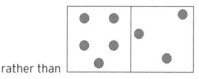

You can still vary the image by using squares rather than dots, or even images of real objects. Keep to one pattern to begin with – e.g. dice patterns or Numicon patterns. It doesn't really matter what pattern you choose as long as you stick with this pattern until the learner is beginning to conceptually subitise, i.e. can combine two smaller sets. Once you feel that the learner is secure in the idea of conceptual subitising and can combine two amounts without counting every individual item, move on to introducing different patterns before moving onto random patterns. For example, you may have started with Steve Chinn's and then moved on to Numicon. Or, you could have used ten frames 'five wise' and then moved on to ten frames 'pairs wise'.

Ensure that you ask the learner how they know how many there are in the frame. For example, did they see 8 as a 4 and a 4 or a 5 and a 3.

In this image the learner can see a 5 and a 3 to make 8.

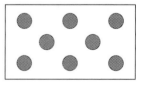

But what about this image? They may see rows of 3, 2 and 3, or they may see different groupings.

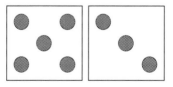

Or this one?

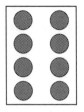

Or this one?

It is interesting to explore the different ways that a learner 'sees' numbers and this will help to develop their number sense and understanding of how that number has been constructed. Once the children can conceptually subitise up to ten, then we can make sure that they can match the numerical quantity to the numerical symbol. This is something that dyscalculic learners will find challenging so don't be afraid to spend a long time on subitising and matching activities.

Pairs

Using a set of digit cards, encourage the learners to match an image (e.g. a dot pattern) to the digit. This can be played as a pairs game.

When the learner is confident in matching the digit to the image then you can introduce matching the digit and the image to the number name.

Dot pattern spinners

Instead of using a standard dice for board games, you can create a spinner that shows random arrangements of dots, digits or number names. This will help learners to make the connection between a numerical symbol, numerical quantity and the number name.

PART/WHOLE REPRESENTATION OF NUMBER AND BUILDING NUMBER SENSE USING NUMBER BONDS

Once the learner can conceptually subitise then the foundations for part/whole thinking have been laid. Learners can now move on to number bonds up to and including 10. These are known as the sight facts and are all the ways that we can make a number from two smaller parts. For example:

$6 = 1 + 5$
$6 = 2 + 4$
$6 = 3 + 3$

We often focus on number bonds to ten, but it is equally as important to know the bonds to all numbers up to ten, as this will help to develop a learner's sense of number and also to enable them to be flexible and efficient in mental calculations.

There are 65 sight facts to be learned, which is a very daunting prospect.

$1 = 0 + 1 = 1 + 0$

$2 = 0 + 2 = 1 + 1 = 2 + 0$

$3 = 0 + 3 = 1 + 2 = 2 + 1 = 3 + 0$

$4 = 0 + 4 = 1 + 3 = 2 + 2 = 3 + 1 = 4 + 0$

$5 = 0 + 5 = 1 + 4 = 2 + 3 = 3 + 2 = 4 + 1 = 5 + 0$

$6 = 0 + 6 = 1 + 5 = 2 + 4 = 3 + 3 = 4 + 2 = 5 + 1 = 6 + 0$

$7 = 0 + 7 = 1 + 6 = 2 + 5 = 3 + 4 = 4 + 3 = 5 + 2 = 6 + 1 = 7 + 0$

$8 = 0 + 8 = 1 + 7 = 2 + 6 = 3 + 5 = 4 + 4 = 5 + 3 = 6 + 2 = 7 + 1 = 8 + 0$

$9 = 0 + 9 = 1 + 8 = 2 + 7 = 3 + 6 = 4 + 5 = 5 + 4 = 6 + 3 = 7 + 2 = 8 + 1 = 9 + 0$

$10 = 0 + 10 = 9 + 1 = 8 + 2 = 7 + 3 = 6 + 4 = 5 + 5 = 4 + 6 = 3 + 7 = 2 + 8 = 1 + 9 = 10 + 0$

An analogy can be made here to learning to read. We have 26 letters in the alphabet and 44 phonemes. We need to know the letter sounds and how letters can be combined in order to be able to read. Similarly, we have 10 digits that make up our number system and the 65 sight facts are the building blocks of maths in the same way that letters and phonemes are the building blocks of literacy. For learners who struggle with basic fact recall we need to find a way to help them make connections between facts so that they don't have to remember them all.

Understanding the commutative property of addition will almost halve the number of facts that have to be recalled. It is even better if these can be taught alongside the corresponding subtraction facts. Teaching the doubles as key facts can be a useful strategy and it is important to teach addition and subtraction alongside each other so that the learners can see the 'permanent' relationship between three numbers.

For example, knowing that $2 + 3 = 5$ means we can derive

$3 + 2 = 5$ (commutative property of addition)
$5 - 2 = 3$ (subtraction as inverse of addition)

and

$5 - 3 = 2$

Five Frame Pelmanism

This activity will develop visualisation, pattern recognition, conservation of number, generalisation and spatial memory. You will need two sets of five frame cards, showing each of the numbers 1 to 5. Place the five frame cards face down in a 2×5 array.

The learner then turns over two cards. If they show the same number of dots, then they can keep that pair. If not, then they are replaced and two more cards are picked. Continue until all five pairs have been found. When you feel that the learner is secure with this then you can move on to numbers to ten. This time you will have a full five frame and the extra counters will be placed on the table outside the five frame. After the learners have had time to work on this then you can introduce the ten frame so that the extra counters have somewhere to go. To begin with, the counters or cubes are arranged in a particular way, filling up each row from left to right. This helps learners to develop a strong visual image of a number quantity and also to understand its relationship to ten. After this is secure then the counters can be arranged in various ways to develop number sense and the conservation of number, for example, understanding that five is still five however it is arranged in the ten frame.

Frame A

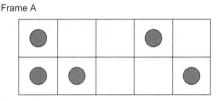

Frame B

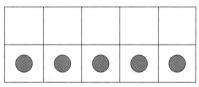

Frame C

Ask the learner to come up with three different ways of placing a set number of counters into a ten frame. How would they describe the counters in Frame A? 3 and 2? Can you see 2+1+1+1? or Can you see 2 + 3? (It depends how you group the counters. Looking across the rows you can see 2 + 3. Looking down the columns you can see 2+1+1+1. Looking for bunches of counters you can see 3 together on the left of the frame and 2 together on the right of the frame.) What about in Frame B? Can you see 4+1? 3+2? How many spaces are there when we have five counters? How do Frame

A and B relate to Frame C? Are they showing the same quantity? The same relationship to ten? Frame C clearly shows that five is half of ten, but this can now be linked to the arrangement in Frame B, showing that halves can be represented in different ways. Learners can clearly see that 7 is 2 more than 5 and 3 less than 10, or that 8 can be seen as '5 plus 3' and as '10 take away 2'.

Learners who have the ability to visualise the numbers one to ten can then work with them more flexibly and will understand the relationship between the numbers. I have found ten frames very helpful in developing automatic recall of number bonds to ten. This is because whenever you see a number represented in the ten frame you also see the complimentary number of spaces that will make ten. So visually, 1 is always linked to 9, 2 is always linked to 8, etc. Often learners will be able to identify a number through the spaces, showing that they have a solid grasp of the addition and subtraction facts to ten.

I have illustrated here some ideas for using ten frames to understand numbers 1 to 10 but we can also use 10 frames to represent other multiples of 10 for example if it was a '1' frame with ten spaces each counter would be worth 0.1 if it was 100 frame each counter would be worth 10 and so on and so forth.

Two-coloured counters

These are one of the most useful resources for teaching sight facts and for part/whole thinking.

For example, when teaching sight facts to 5 we can set the counters out like this.

$5 - 0 = 5$	$5 + 0 = 5$
$5 - 1 = 4$	$4 + 1 = 5$
$5 - 2 = 3$	$3 + 2 = 5$
$5 - 3 = 2$	$2 + 3 = 5$
$5 - 4 = 1$	$1 + 4 = 5$
$5 - 5 = 0$	$0 + 5 = 5$

Or we can set them out like the 5 on a dice.

By turning over the centre counter we can see that the dice pattern of 5 is made from the dice pattern of 1 and the dice pattern of 4.

By turning over the two diagonals we can see that the dice pattern of 5 is made from the dice pattern of 2 and the dice pattern of 3.

These visuals can really help learners to develop their knowledge of sight facts.

We can also use ten frames to illustrate the sight facts.

Start with the doubles.

For example – double 3 = 6

Using two-coloured counters we can emphasise on the ten frame that we have two equal rows of counters.

We can see that double numbers are even.

Now we can start deriving new facts by using near doubles.

3 + 4 = 7

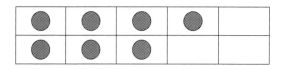

3 + 2 = 5

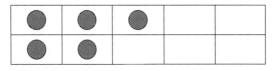

Coloured cubes

Cubes are a resource that are in every primary classroom. When teaching early maths concepts make sure that the cubes you use are all the same shape size and colour. This helps to make the concept you are teaching clearer as there is no 'distracting variable' for learners. Cubes are often used for counting and sorting in early years but can also be used later on for more sophisticated modelling, such as bar modelling or in ratio and fraction work.

Number stories

This activity will help to develop number sense, to understand the conservation of number and that addition and subtraction are inverse operations. First of all, decide on the number that you want to work with; for example, 5. Ask the learner to make a tower of 5 blue cubes. Ask them to count the cubes and tell you how many there are. Now replace one blue cube with a red. Then ask:

How many cubes do you have altogether? How many blue cubes? How many red cubes? So what does 4 and 1 make? What is 5 – 1? What is 5 – 4? We can repeat this process by swapping one blue cube for a red cube, until all the cubes are red. Each time we are creating a concrete representation and the children can record this both pictorially and in symbolic form.

Below is the number story for 5 that we will have created.

5 + 0 = 5
5 - 0 = 5
4 + 1 = 5
5 - 1 = 4
3 + 2 = 5

5 - 2 = 3
2 + 3 = 5
5 - 3 = 2
1 + 4 = 5
5 - 4 = 1
0 + 5 = 5
5 - 0 = 5
5 - 5 = 0

NUMBER BONDS TO NUMBERS UP TO 10

This will help with part/whole thinking, composition of number and decomposition, as well as recall of number facts for numbers up to 10. This activity follows on from previous one and again you will need to decide what number you are focusing on. For illustration, I will choose 8.

Ask the learner to make a tower of eight cubes (all the same colour). Now take the tower and hold it behind your back. Break off a section of cubes. Show this section to the learner and ask them: 'How many cubes are behind my back?' Repeat the exercise and take it in turns so that the learners can do the hiding as well. This activity will develop their visualisation, their visual and auditory memory as well as giving them practice in breaking numbers down into different parts. Repeat this for all the different bonds to eight and make sure that each one is recorded pictorially and in symbols.

CUISENAIRE RODS

Cuisenarie rods were devised in the 1920s by Georges Cuisenaire, a Belgian educator. They became popular in the 1950s through the work of Caleb Gattegno. Cuisenaire rods consist of a set of rods, made of wood or plastic in ten different colours ranging in size from 1 cm to 10 cm long. The rods are not marked into units and this is where their strength lies. Since they are not marked into units, they are useful for developing mathematical reasoning and number sense and encourage learners to move away from counting in ones. The original wooden rods were weighted, so for example, the 3 and the 4 rods together would weigh the same as the 7 rod. The colours were also chosen to help develop understanding of number relationships.

Colours

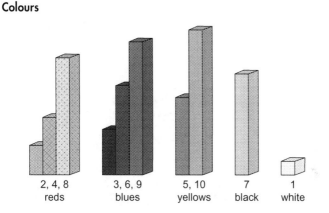

| 2, 4, 8 | 3, 6, 9 | 5, 10 | 7 | 1 |
| reds | blues | yellows | black | white |

The 1 rod is white/cream as this is the most universal count-ing rod. The 7 rod is black because it does not have a double or half relationship with any of the other rods The remaining rods are grouped into three families according to the primary colours, red, yellow and blue. The inspiration for these rods came from musical analogies. Cuisenaire was curious as to why learners understood music more easily than maths. The stair-case formation, when the rods are placed in increasing order of length, was inspired by Pan pipes.

When introducing any manipulative for the first time let the learners explore and play with the new manipulative. Research from Zoltan Dienes has shown us that learners need plenty of experience of this informal exploration before they have any formal mathematical instruction. The possibilities are endless but here are some examples:

Building a staircase pattern.

Making squares of rectangles.

Standing the rods upright or making towers of different heights or pictures of your choice.

Create repeating patterns.

Once the learners have had time to play and discover the new manipulative then you can start introducing more formal activities and structured games. The staircase game is very good for ordering numbers 1 to 10 and subsequently placing them on a number line.

Staircase Game

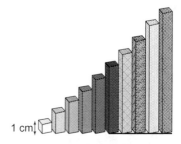

1 cm

Players take it in turns to roll a 1–10 dice and place the corresponding Cuisenaire Rod on the table to create a sequence. If your number is repeated when the dice is thrown you have to miss a turn. If Player 1 throws a 5 they will place the yellow rod on the table. If Player 2 then throws a 7 they will have to decide how far to the right of the 5 to place the 7 rod in order to make a staircase. This game encourages children to think about the relative value of the numbers 1 to 10 and to appreciate the distance between two numbers on a number line.

If you wanted to explore the concept of part/whole thinking then you could use the rods to make rod sandwiches.

Rod Sandwiches

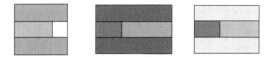

Decide what number you want to be your whole and then select two of those rods. Sandwich the two rods together and then fill the sandwich with a combination of two other rods. This can be extended to filling the sandwich with three or even four rods. You can also do this by starting with a 7, 8, 9 or 10 rod sandwich and then rolling a standard dice to find the first 'filling' rod. Can the learner tell you what rod is needed to complete the filling?

If you want to move on to exploring repeated addition and multiplication then you can use the rods to make trains and arrays.

Train Game

In this activity, we are exploring multiplication as repeated addition and also looking at the factors of a number. If our target number is 10 then we can explore how many identical rods are needed to make a train the same length as the 10 rod. This image tells us that

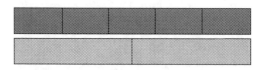

$2+2+2+2+2=10$ and also that $5+5=10$

If we now make a 10 rod with ten 1 rods (in other words, the small cube) we can see that 1, 2, 5 and 10 are the factors of 10.

Arrays

By using the rods to make rectangles we can demonstrate the commutative property of multiplication. In this image, you can see that three of the five rods make a rectangle that is exactly the same size as a rectangle made from five of the three rods.

Number stories

We can also use the rods to tell the story of a number. The story of a number is all the number bonds that make that number. This image tells the story of 10 and also demonstrates the commutative property of addition.

There are many more mathematical concepts that can be illustrated using Cuisenaire rods. In fact they can be used for teaching pretty much any aspect of maths from early years to adult level and are one of the most sophisticated and versatile manipulatives available.

Diene's blocks have been around for a similar length of time to Cuisenaire rods and are commonly used in all primary schools. Often referred to as base-10 materials, they are the 'go to' manipulative when working with place value.

BASE-10 MATERIALS

Base-10 materials are a proportionate manipulative. The 10 rod is 10 times the size of the 1 cube. The 100 flat is 10 times the size of the 10 rod. The 1,000-large cube is 10 times the size of the 100 flat. For some dyscalculic learners the sophistication and versatility of Cuisenaire rods makes them inaccessible. They may prefer to work with base-10 materials, which are always multiples of 10. However, in the world of dyscalculia there are two camps. Some practitioners prefer to work with Cuisenaire rods because of their versatility. You will find books by experts such as Ronit Bird almost exclusively modelling maths using Cuisenaire rods. Other practitioners prefer the consistency and proportionality of base-10 materials. In my experience it depends on the learner that you are working with. Try modelling the concept with both base-10 and Cuisenaire rods and see which one the learner responds to best.

If in your school you have the original wooden Dienes blocks, they have an advantage over the more modern plastic version. The fact that they are wooden gives them weight so that the 1,000 cube is very heavy indeed and this helps the children to conceptualise the magnitude of 1,000 compared to one. Furthermore, the fact that they are wooden means that they're all the same colour and learners have to focus on the relative size of the materials rather than any colour. The more modern materials use different colours for the ones, rods, flats and 1,000 cube, leading to some learners remembering the colour over the relative magnitude.

SUMMARY

- Spend time on the foundations of maths: matching, sorting and our counting system.
- Use manipulatives to help learners build up then knowledge of sight facts.
- Encourage children to move on from counting towards part/ whole thinking.

8

SPECIFIC STRATEGIES
FOR KEY STAGE 2

Traditionally as learners move from Key Stage 1 to Key Stage 2, maths teaching becomes more abstract, and manipulatives are used less. It comes as no surprise then that this transition from Key Stage 1 to Key Stage 2 is the point at which teachers notice learners beginning to give up on maths. Often, where manipulatives are used, they are thought of as a means of supporting learners who are struggling and have a certain stigma attached to them. It can be quite a challenge to persuade learners that they should be using them as a matter of course and that they will benefit all learners, not just the ones who are struggling. This chapter will focus on the use of a range of manipulatives that will support dyscalculic learners but they should be made available to all children as this will help to take the stigma away from their use.

Another problem that comes to the fore in Key Stage 2 is difficulty with word problems and this chapter will also look at strategies to help learners to decipher and solve word problems, such as Bar Modelling and numberless word problems.

MANIPULATIVES FOR KEY STAGE 2

TWO-COLOURED COUNTERS

Not just for use in Key Stage 1, two-coloured counters can be used for a wide range of Key Stage 2 topics. Here we are going to look at algebra and zero pairs.

When children are introduced to letters representing numbers, this can be a real barrier to their understanding. However, algebraic thinking is a concept that learners will have been

DOI: 10.4324/9781003326625-10

introduced to from quite an early age, when they have to fill in blank spaces or empty boxes. The problem begins when we use letters to represent numbers. I was working with a learner who professed that he was OK with maths until the alphabet got involved. If we use two-coloured counters in place of letters such as X and Y, it can take away the abstract nature of using letters for numbers and also take away some of the fear. It makes the maths much more accessible.

For example, if I have two blue counters and one red counter and I say to the learner,

> *What could the value of the counters be if when we add them together you get 10? The blue counters have to have the same value because they are the same colour and the red counter could have a different value.*

Try this for yourself!

You may come up with the following solutions.

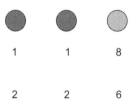

| 1 | 1 | 8 |
| 2 | 2 | 6 |

Etc.

Actually there are an infinite number of solutions to this problem because I didn't stipulate that we needed whole numbers. You could have fractions or decimals or even negative numbers in your solution. Effectively what we have done is solved the equation

$$2x + y = 10$$

but by using the two-coloured counters we have made it much more accessible to the learner and much less threatening.

Another use of two-coloured counters is for zero pairs. A zero pair is where you have one counter that has the value of plus one and the other counter has the value of negative one. When you put them together they make 0. Working with negative numbers is something that children often struggle with. We teach it in a procedural way by saying a minus and a minus makes a plus. They just learn these little phrases but they don't really understand what's happening.

Let's say our blue counter is 1 and our red counter is negative 1.

What would -3 + 2 = ?

Lay out 3 of the red counters and line up underneath with 2 of the blue counters. Circle all the 0 pairs. We can remove these as their value is 0.

We are left with the answer -1.

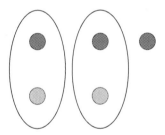

In the next example we are looking at 6 plus -2. We have two zero pairs here leaving us with 4.

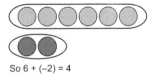

So 6 + (−2) = 4

In this example, we are taking 5 away from 4. In order to do this, we need to add some zero pairs. We have added three zero pairs here but in fact we only needed one. It doesn't matter as the extra ones have a value of 0, so they won't change the answer. What they do help us with is to see how we can take 5 away from 4. The answer is ⁻1.

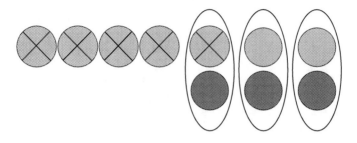

TACKLING WORD PROBLEMS

Often it is the interpretation of the word problem that is the issue, rather than the maths itself. The dyscalculic learner may have difficulty in understanding the problem and also in carrying out the correct calculation.

In terms of vocabulary, there are some words that are only used in maths lessons, for example numerator and denominator, and this can lead to a perceived disconnect between maths and the real world. As much as possible, we need to link the maths and the word problems that we use to the real world, but we also need to make sure that the contexts are realistic. We have all seen word problems where someone buys 24 melons, but this isn't really a realistic context for young children. One way to help children make this connection between maths and the real world is to get them to create their own word problems and to encourage them to reflect on whether it is a realistic problem. For example, sharing some money between two siblings is believable, but sharing money between 22 siblings is not realistic.

Asking children to create their own word problems also helps them to develop their use of precise mathematical terminology.

We need to make sure that we emphasise the importance of prepositions in word problems. These small words can often be overlooked when a learner is reading a word problem, particularly if the context and the names used are overly complex. You can see that 'divide 25 by 10' and 'divide 25 into 10' are completely different calculations but look very similar. Another example would be 'reduce this price by £20' and 'reduce this price to £20'. Again, completely different maths. Sometimes in word problems there are ambiguities; we are not always as precise with our use of mathematical language as we should be. Consider the following questions:

What is 10 divided into 5? (2 or 0.5).

How much is 5 more than 3? (2 or 8).

Another problem that learners have are miscues in word problems. Look at this example.

Jack has 10 apples. He had 7 *more* than Mary. How many apples did Mary have?

The word more is leading the learner to think that this is an addition question, whereas the operation that we actually need to do is subtraction. In order to help learners tackle word problems effectively they need to have experience of problem-solving strategies. In the 1950s George Polya wrote a seminal book, called *How to Solve It*. In this book he set out the strategies for solving a problem. These were to:

- Understand the problem.
- Plan how you are going to tackle the problem.
- Solve the problem.
- Look back at your solution and check.

Newman's Procedure adds to this and is a useful framework for practitioners to identify the barriers to understanding word problems that individual learners may have.

This procedure identifies difficulties that may occur at any stage of the problem-solving process.

NEWMAN'S PROCEDURE

Australian educator Anne Newman (1977) suggested five prompts to help determine where errors may occur in student's attempts to solve written problems.

Students make mistakes for many reasons. Teachers will be familiar with mistakes due to reading and comprehension problems. Newman also identified transformation, process skills and encoding.

Research in Australia and South East Asia showed that 60% of students' errors in responding to written numeracy questions occur before students reach the process skills level. In contrast, most remediation programs focus solely on the process skills.

NEWMAN'S FIVE PROMPTS

Reading

Can the learner read the words in the problem? Even good readers can find it difficult to read and decode mathematical texts, words and graphics.

When reading a word problem, are the learners reading for meaning?

The following question is an example that illustrates many learners are not reading for meaning. This was given to a group of children and their responses were recorded.

> There are 26 sheep and 10 chickens on a farm. How old is the farmer?

78% of children did one of the following:

$$26 + 10 = 36$$
$$26 - 10 = 16$$
$$26 \times 10 = 260$$
$$26 \div 10 = 2.6$$

Now you could argue that is a trick question, but it illustrates a lack of reading for meaning. We need to encourage children to read the problem out loud, to miss out any words that they can't read and to highlight any words that they don't know. They can work with a reading partner and use maths word charts for support in the classroom. They can swap names for generic nouns or pronouns to make reading the problem more accessible.

Comprehension

Is reading comprehension the difficulty? Can the learner understand the meaning of what they are reading? Learners may be able to decode the words but at the expense of comprehension. They may not understand the meaning of the words and graphics in a mathematical context. They may confuse the everyday meanings of words and substitute this for mathematical contexts. Learners need to identify what information is important and what is irrelevant. This is so much more complicated than just highlighting the key words! If you are able to highlight what is important it doesn't mean you know why it's important or what you need to do with that information. What if you think everything is important? This will prevent them from building an understanding of what the question is asking them to do.

Learners may read the problem only once and may take an incorrect meaning from the words or they may be put off and distracted by the numbers, especially if there are large numbers in the problem. We can help learners with comprehension difficulties by encouraging them to look for key maths vocabulary, to question and monitor their understanding of the problem. We can show them how to break the problem down into smaller steps and to see the connection with similar problems that they have completed before. The use of the Bar Model is incredibly powerful in helping learners to visualise the problem and to understand what the problem is asking them to do.

Transformation

Can the learner determine a way to solve the problem? Does the learner have a good knowledge of strategies? Can they transform the written word into the calculation that they need to do? Can they actually carry out that calculation correctly and are they able to check their answer using a different method?

If the problem is how to transform the words of a problem into an appropriate mathematical strategy to solve the problem, then they can employ some of Polya's strategies to do this, including:

- Draw a picture.
- Guess and check.
- Act it out – using manipulatives.
- Write a number sentence.
- Find a pattern.
- Make an orderly list.
- Eliminate the possibilities.
- Work backwards.

Representing the problem with a diagram; for example, a Bar Model can be a game changer. Using numberless word problems is also another highly effective approach.

Furthermore, if learners are encouraged to write their own word problems, they will become more familiar with the structure and meaning of the word problem, encourage them to present word problems in different ways using different vocabulary and use problems that reflect different models of the four operations.

Processing skills

Can the learner engage in the mathematical process? Most teachers are excellent at teaching math skills such as multiplication, addition, division and subtraction and learners are able to follow the process of these skills. The problem arises if they do not know when to apply these skills. Most students do not know which operational process is required to solve a problem. Again, the Bar Model can be extremely powerful here helping the learner to see what operation they need to use. Using Polya's strategies at the transformation stage will help the learner to determine what the mathematical process needs to be.

Encoding

Can the learner record and interpret their answer in relation to the problem?

Can they test that the answer is correct? How can they be sure?

Learners need to reflect on their answer and ask themselves the following questions

- Does it make sense?
- Does it answer what the question is asking?
- Is the answer close to my estimation?

Having the structure of Polya's strategies to problem-solving and Newman's prompts will provide learners with a framework to support them when tackling word problems. It will also enable practitioners to find out where the barriers to solving the word problems are. It may be one or two of the prompts in Newman's procedure or it may be all five! Having the knowledge of where the problems lie enables us to find a solution and a way of supporting the learner more effectively.

BAR MODELLING

The Bar Model method for problem-solving was introduced in the 1980s to help students who were struggling with word problems in maths. It has proven to be so successful that its use is now spreading across the world as more teachers and learners discover how powerful it can be in helping students to 'see the maths'. It is effectively acting as a bridge between the word problem and the abstract maths. The Bar Model exposes the relationships within the structure of the mathematics and supports the development of algebraic thinking.

There are three different types of model:

- The Part/Whole Model.
- The Comparison Model.
- The Before and After Model.

THE PART/WHOLE MODEL

Initially the Part/Whole Model is used to represent simple addition problems. For example: Jack has five pencils and Jay has eight pencils. How many pencils do they have altogether?

Concrete objects can be used to model this problem: real pencils or pictures of pencils or cubes to represent the pencils.

Bars (or rectangles) are drawn to represent the problem. The bars don't need to be exactly in proportion but just need to look reasonable in terms of relative size. Brackets are used to show the given information and also for the unknown. The question mark tells us what we are trying to find out and what calculation we need to do.

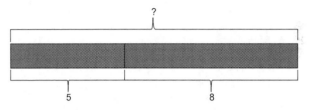

The two parts are added together giving the whole.

5 + 8 = 13

There are 13 pencils altogether.

In this example we knew the two parts and had to find the whole. It may be that the given information is the whole and one part and the learner needs to find the other part. In this case the operation would be subtraction of one part from the whole to find the other part as shown in the example below.

The calculation here would be 61 take away 33 to find the number of boys at the party.

There were 61 children at the party. 33 of them were girls. How many boys were there?

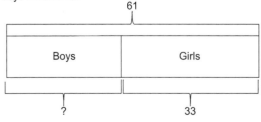

THE COMPARISON MODEL

In the Comparison Model, two quantities are compared. For example, there are ten apples and six bananas. How many more apples are there than bananas? This can be modelled as follows:

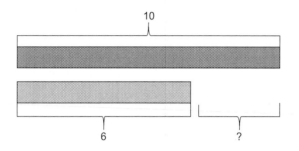

The Bar Model shows us that we need to subtract:

10 - 6 = 4

There are four more apples than bananas.

It may be that we are given one amount and the difference. The model will still be the same.

There are four more apples than bananas. If there are six bananas, how many apples are there?

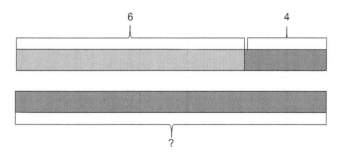

The Bar Model is the same, it is just the information given that is different and for this problem we need to add:

6 + 4 = 10

There are ten apples.

THE BEFORE AND AFTER MODEL

In before and after problems there are two models. One for the situation before the change (an increase or decrease in quantity) and one for the situation after the change.

Sunil has fives times as much money as Jack. Sunil gives Jack £10 and now they both have the same amount. How much money did Sunil have to begin with?

Before model

Sunil

Jack

10

Sunil must have given two parts to Jack for them to have the same amount at the end. Each part must therefore be 5.

After model

Sunil

Jack

So at the beginning Sunil must have had £25

In all my years of teaching, discovering the Bar Model has to be one of my biggest 'wow' moments. It is a complete game changer for many children, particularly those with dyscalculia and dyslexia. Its use is a lot more prevalent in primary schools now and with good reason. You may find learners initially reluctant to draw the Bar Model as they see it as an extra step, but once they have realised how helpful it can be in terms of solving word problems they will soon be converted. For young children, or children who are not happy drawing the rectangles, you can use strips of paper, counters or cubes. These are particularly useful when you are working on before and after problems because you can move things around to model the change in the problem. I expect a lot of you will already be using the Bar Model but if you are not I cannot recommend it highly enough.

SUMMARY

- Manipulatives are useful for children of all ages and not just those in Key Stage 1.
- Make them readily available to all children to avoid any stigma attached to their use.
- Word problems will be more accessible through the use of Polya and Newman's frameworks as well as the Bar Model.

9

WORKING WITH PARENTS

Parents can be one of our greatest resources when it comes to supporting learners with dyscalculia or maths learning difficulties, but it can be hard to get them on board, particularly if they have their own anxieties about maths. Many parents feel that they don't want to get involved in case they confuse their child further, or are afraid that they won't be able to do the maths themselves and are reluctant for their child to see them struggling as well. It can also be upsetting for parents to find out that their child has a specific learning difference, and this may make them feel that they are even more unlikely to be able to help. They may well think that it is best left to the professionals!

So, the first thing that we need to do is to get them engaged and also to help them, and their child, to develop more of a growth mindset when it comes to maths. You may decide to work individually with parents or to have whole class activities that involve the parents. Or you may wish to start off by sending home simple information sheets or even questionnaires.

The earlier that we can get the parents involved the better the outcome will be for the child. The ways that they can help at home are plentiful and non-threatening. We are not necessarily asking them to do lots of worksheets with the learners; far from it! What we are aiming for is to get the parent and child enjoying maths together, and this doesn't even have to be related to the curriculum or the area of maths that they are struggling with. Maths is such a diverse and fascinating subject, and we often bypass some of the best bits in our quest (and from the pressure) to get through the curriculum. Maths in school is bound by the demands of the curriculum and is performance-driven, but maths at home doesn't have to be any of those things.

DOI: 10.4324/9781003326625-11

INCIDENTAL MATHS

There is a lot of maths that learners and parents are doing every day, without really noticing it, and this is a good starting point for developing enthusiasm for maths and taking away some of the fear.

Some examples may include:

- When brushing the teeth, ask the child to estimate how long they have brushed for. Now time them and find out how close their estimate was to the actual time. This can be a reminder that two minutes is longer than they think!
- Laying the table for breakfast/dinner will reinforce 1:1 correspondence. How many plates will we need if two more people join us?
- Counting forwards each step as we go upstairs and backwards as we go downstairs will help to get the order of our number system, or you can literally step count forwards and backwards in twos, fives and tens, or whatever is appropriate for the child.
- On the walk to school, can they identify odd numbers and even numbers in the environment, on houses, on buses?

HOMEWORK

Rather than giving homework for a dyscalculic learner to do with their parents who may have their own issues with maths it can be more beneficial to send home games and explorations. These can be a great way of practising the maths that has been taught in school in a fun and non-threatening way. It can also help to dispel maths anxiety in the parents and their children. You may also decide to send home activities that are not based on topics that have been covered in school and are just for fun to develop a sense of curiosity. During the pandemic I posted every day on Twitter an activity for parents to do with their children and have included one of my favourite examples below.

THE MOBIUS STRIP

You will need

and sticky tape.

The Mobius Strip is named after the mathematician August Mobius who invented the strip in 1858. It is curious because it only has one side and one edge. A Mobius Strip is simple to construct. All you need is a long strip of paper, sticky tape and a pair of scissors.

If you have A4 printer paper you can cut two strips about 5 cm in width and tape them together. That will give you a strip that's about the right length.

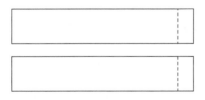

Once you have a long strip you can now tape the ends together as if you were making a headband.

Try drawing a line along the middle of the headband, on the inside and on the outside.

Could you do this without taking the pen off the paper?

No, because the strip of paper (and therefore the headband) has two sides.

But now try this ...

Take another long piece of paper and match the ends together as if you were making a headband, *but* before you attach the two ends with tape, give one of them a twist and then stick the ends together.

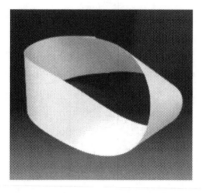

Now try drawing a line along the centre of the strip. What do you notice?

You will end up back where you started, without having to take your pen off the paper. So, you have drawn on both sides of the strip of paper in one go, meaning that your original strip of paper, which had two sides, now only has one side!

How is that possible?

Now cut along the line that you have drawn. What do you think might happen?

Try it and see!

There are many other interesting things that you can do with this strip. Try making another one, but this time instead of cutting along the middle, cut a third of the way from one edge. What do you think will happen this time?

What happens if you make two twists in the paper? Or even three twists?

Have fun exploring this and see if you can predict what will happen!

HOW TO EXPLAIN DYSCALCULIA TO A PARENT

This can be a very tricky conversation to have. Some parents may be very resistant to the idea that their child has a learning difference. If you have a straightforward explanation to give them and a plan for how you are going to support their child, it can help immensely. You may want to give them an information sheet or you may want to sit down and have a conversation with them. Something along the following lines should help.

Dyscalculia is a specific learning difference in mathematics that affects around 5% of the population. It is really a difficulty in arithmetic, rather than in maths as a whole, as there may be no difficulty with topics such as shape or geometry. Dyscalculic people have difficulty matching an amount to the symbol we use for that amount. When they see the symbol 5, they don't have a picture of five items in their mind. Consequently, they struggle with identifying which of two numbers is the larger. They also lack number sense, which means that they find it hard to understand our system of counting and how numbers relate to each other. They will have difficulty doing calculations in their head.

Dyscalculia is present from birth and is a lifelong condition that is totally unrelated to IQ. Having dyscalculia does not mean that your child has low intelligence. Often far from it! The effects of dyscalculia can be lessened with good intervention and support, which your child will be receiving in school. (You can detail here exactly what your school is doing to support their child, such as extra time in tests or exams, or having individual or small group learning support.) Try to reassure the parent that this does not mean that their child will never be able to do maths. It does not need to be a barrier to success. Emphasise the importance of making maths part of everyday life but in a fun and non-threatening way. It is important that any parental anxiety is not transferred to their child.

You may want to go into more detail about the specific things that their child may struggle with and you can also highlight the strengths that their child may have as a result of their dyscalculia.

Dyscalculic learners will struggle with the following.

UNDERSTANDING NUMBER

They may not know that 9 is more than 5, because they have not attached a quantity to the number. To them, 9 is a symbol that we call 'nine' but it does not conjure up an image of nine items.

SUBITISING

Subitising is our ability to say how many items there are in a set without actually counting them. Most people, when looking at four biscuits on a plate would be able to say instantly there were four without counting them. A dyscalculic person does not have this automatic recognition of small quantities and would have to count the biscuits.

ESTIMATION

Dyscalculic learners don't have a feel for what the answer may be, so they will accept whatever number they come up with. For example, we know that 34 + 62 is almost 100 but a dyscalculic person may end up with the answer 3,462 and not realise that this must be incorrect.

COUNTING BACKWARDS

Numbers are just words to a dyscalculic person so counting backwards has no logical structure. They may be able to recite the sequence forwards but have no idea why one number comes after another. Try reciting a familiar nursery rhyme backwards to get a sense of how difficult counting backwards can be for someone with dyscalculia.

SPOTTING PATTERNS

Being able to spot patterns can make maths a whole lot easier, but dyscalculic people find this very hard.

For example:

10 + 4 = 14
20 + 4 = 24
30 + 4 = 34
40 + 4 = 44

We can see a pattern emerging here, but a dyscalculic child would not see that the next answer will be 54.

UNDERSTANDING PLACE VALUE

This is a tricky concept for many young learners but particularly hard for dyscalculic learners who find it hard to understand that the digit can change value depending on its place in the number. Dyscalculic people will often write 1002 instead of 102 when they hear one hundred and two, because they have not understood the concept of place value and they write the symbols to maths the words that they hear.

TIME

Learning to tell the time is notoriously difficult and many learners will struggle with this, dyscalculic learners particularly so. However, it is not only telling the time that is challenging but also understanding the passage of time. A dyscalculic person may not be able to appreciate whether an hour has passed or only a few minutes.

Dyscalculic learners may have strengths in the following areas.

CREATIVITY

Many dyscalculic learners are creative and this is often due to the imaginative ways that they have had to develop to overcome their issues with number. This creativity can also lead to high-level skills in strategic thinking and problem solving. These are skills that are highly valued in the workplace today.

LITERACY

Often, dyscalculic people will have an excellent memory for the printed word and may excel in language learning and poetry.

PERSEVERANCE AND RESILIENCE

Dyscalculic learners will have to work harder than their peers and with the right support and encouragement this can lead to them developing resilience and perseverance. These are great life skills which will serve them well as they progress into adulthood.

Dyscalculia need not be a barrier to achieving your potential. A couple of years ago I had the great pleasure of meeting Aidan Milner in New Zealand. He is severely dyslexic and dyscalculic but had worked hard at overcoming these difficulties and at the time was doing a Master's degree in Geology as well as volunteering for the ambulance service on a Friday night. He is an incredibly accomplished young man and a testament to the fact that you can achieve success in life even with a specific learning difference.

Professor Paul Moorcraft was a BBC correspondent and was described by Professor Brian Butterworth (a leading researcher in dyscalculia) as the most dyscalculic person he had ever assessed. Paul is a Professor of Journalism and Media, a former BBC war correspondent and the author of 25 books.

SUMMARY

- Parents can be one of our greatest resources.
- Be positive when explaining dyscalculia.
- Detail the support that will be provided in school.
- Explain clearly how the parent can help their child.

10

PLANNING FOR TRANSITION

Transition from primary to secondary can be a challenging time for any learner, but particularly for neurodiverse learners. In primary school, children are used to having one class teacher, who will know them very well and will have a good understanding of their learning needs. However, in secondary school they will have different subject teachers who are working with many classes and the opportunity to get to know every child individually and in depth is more limited.

Communication is the key thing here. The transition will be much smoother if there are good lines of communication between parents, learners, primary teachers and secondary teachers.

GUIDANCE FOR TRANSITION

Remember that all teachers will need to know about a learner's dyscalculia, not just their maths teacher. As awareness of dyscalculia is still quite low, it may be a good idea to offer a staff meeting to the secondary school where you can explain how to identify and support learners with dyscalculia, or at the very least offer a short explanation of it and how it may affect the learner.

Explain what support the learner has been given in primary school, whether it has been 1:1 intervention or support within the class. What support strategies have worked best for the learner?

Demonstrate the manipulatives that the learner has been using. If the learner is used to having Numicon to hand, there is a secondary-age version of this that is grey in colour. This can help the learner to feel that they are not still having to rely

DOI: 10.4324/9781003326625-12

on manipulatives that they consider to be for primary-aged children.

Make sure that they are not going to be given copious amounts of worksheets. The focus needs to be on the concrete and pictorial. If concrete manipulatives are not available, then virtual ones are the next best thing: www.mathsbot.com is a fantastic website for virtual manipulatives created by a secondary maths teacher, Jonathan Hall.

Prepare the learner early, have frequent visits to the new school and give the learner samples of activities that they will be doing in maths. These would ideally be game-based and something that the learner can do with their parents or siblings.

New teachers can't assume that all primary maths has been mastered. They will need to constantly reinforce concepts, be patient and expect less completed homework. Before any new topic is introduced make sure that the learner has the pre-requisite knowledge to access that new topic.

Try to make abstract concepts such as algebra visual through the use of the Bar Model and two-coloured counters to represent the unknown quantity rather than letters of the alphabet.

If the learner appears withdrawn or is displaying challenging behaviour, consider as a first point of call whether maths anxiety is the issue.

SUMMARY

- Communication is key.
- Make sure the learner is prepared.

11

FURTHER RESOURCES

WHAT TO DO IF YOU SUSPECT DYSCALCULIA

Dyscalculia is legally recognised as a disability. This means that schools have an obligation to identify learners with dyscalculia and to put in place reasonable adjustments to ensure that these learners have the same opportunities as every other child in the class.

I am often asked at what age you can diagnose dyscalculia. My advice to any teacher would be to look out for the learner who is not progressing at the same rate as their peers. This is not always easy to do, especially in Key Stage 1 when the impact of being an August or a September birthday can be quite profound.

However, it is not so much about labelling and diagnosis at this stage as being aware of learners not reaching typical developmental milestones.

If you are concerned, then the first step would be to complete a checklist. This can give you a better idea as to whether the learner is not keeping up with their peers and in what areas.

CHECKLISTS

Checklists are simple and quick to administer and are often the first option to take when trying to identify dyscalculia. However, they can be very subjective and will only ever give an indication of whether the learner is at risk of dyscalculia.

There are many checklists for dyscalculia that can either be purchased or accessed free online including:

- The British Dyslexia Association Checklist for Dyscalculia: www.bdadyslexia.org.
- Ann Arbor Dyscalculia Checklist: www.annarbor.co.uk.

DOI: 10.4324/9781003326625-13

- More Trouble with Maths by Steve Chinn includes a 31-point checklist: www.stevechinn.co.uk.
- The Mathematics Shed has a more comprehensive checklist that is divided into the following areas: number system, calculations, solving problems, measures, shape and space and handling data. www.mathematicshed.com.

The next stage would be to carry out a screener for dyscalculia.

SCREENERS

The screener will give you an idea if that child is at risk of dyscalculia. At this stage you may decide to intervene and give extra support to the learner, and this will most often be best placed within the whole class environment. Make sure that you are following the dyscalculia-friendly classroom guidance, as this will be beneficial for all learners. The one thing that we need to avoid is waiting for the child to fail before we take action. If there is even the slightest hint of potential dyscalculia, then we should be looking at employing strategies to provide extra support. At this stage, I would recommend having a conversation with the parents of the learner. This should be an informal discussion, where I would not use the term dyscalculia specifically, but I would be giving them suggestions for ways that they can give their child extra support at home.

NUMERACY SCREENER

www.numeracyscreener.org.
Age range: 4–8 years.
This is a two-minute screening test to identify children who are struggling in maths. The test itself will not be able to identify dyscalculia per se, but it will highlight those children who may need extra input or more careful monitoring. The test is free and very easy to administer. It can be downloaded at numeracyscreener.org, along with test instructions. The children are required to identify which of two numbers or symbols are larger on a series of worksheets. They answer as many questions as they can in two minutes.
Cost: free.

DYNAMO ASSESSMENT

www.dynamoprofiler.co.uk.

Age range: 6–11 years.

This screening tool has been developed by Dynamo Maths, a company that offer online intervention activities for learners with dyscalculia and maths difficulties. The Dynamo Maths profiler is a simple online test that will identify specific areas of difficulty, in particular individual variation in number sense development. It takes between 20 and 40 minutes to complete.

The results are displayed in a bar chart and cover:

- Speed of processing.
- Number meaning.
- Number relationships.
- Number magnitude.

This screener is particularly useful as it produces two reports: a Number Sense Profile Report and a Performance Profile Report.

The Number Sense Profile report distinguishes between dyscalculic difficulties and developmental delay in maths.

The Performance Profile Report gives a detailed view of the child's strengths and weaknesses and signposts intervention strategies to support them.

Cost: ~ £15 per child.

THE DYSCALCULIA SCREENER

www.gl-assessment.co.uk.

Age range: 6–14 years.

The screener identifies dyscalculic tendencies and provides a report which recommends intervention strategies for support. An accompanying book, Dyscalculia Guidance, is available that details games and activities for such intervention. The test takes around 30 minutes and can be used individually or as a whole class screener. It aims to help practitioners distinguish between those individuals who have poor maths attainment and those whose difficulties are associated with dyscalculia. It assesses the learner's sense of number through evaluating their ability to understand number size and how well they perform simple calculations.

Cost: £5.50 (+VAT) per individual administration (for a minimum of 10 administrations).

DYSCALCULIA SCREENER

https://idlsgroup.com/idl-numeracy-screener.
Age range: 4–11 years.
This screener has been developed to provide a simple-to-use online test that will highlight any dyscalculic tendencies. The test takes around 15 minutes and can be used to screen an entire group or for individual pupils.

Cost: free.

DIAGNOSTIC ASSESSMENT OF NUMERACY SKILLS (DANS)

www.senbooks.co.uk/product/diagnostic-assessment-of -numeracy-skills-dans-.
Age range: 5–11 years.
This assessment enables specialist maths teachers to determine areas of numerical strength and weakness in their students, facilitating intervention and the writing of Individual Maths Development Plans. The activities are concrete-based with many games and allow the students to really show what they know. The assessment is laid out as two separate 1-hour lessons but can easily be given as 4 30-minute lessons. As this is not a standardised test it can be adapted to meet your students' needs.

Cost: £160.00 + VAT.

INFORMAL ASSESSMENT

There are also two books that I would particularly recommend that can be very helpful in building a more detailed profile of a learner's difficulties with maths.

DYSCALCULIA ASSESSMENT BY JANE EMERSON AND PATRICIA BABTIE

This very useful book will help practitioners to identify which aspects of numeracy the child is struggling to acquire. The evidence from the assessment can then be used to draw up a personalized teaching plan. It is ideal for use with primary school children but can also be adapted for use with older children.

The book is written in a very clear way with step-by-step instructions and photocopiable assessment sheets that help in formulating individual intervention programmes. It contains guidance on how to conduct the assessments, including suggested scripts, teaching tips and strategies as well as instructions on interpretation of the results and a range of motivating games and activities.

MORE TROUBLE WITH MATHS *BY STEVE CHINN*

This is a highly practical, easy-to-use book which covers assessment of a wide range of factors. Steve Chinn draws on his extensive experience and expertise to:

- Show how to consider all the factors relating to mathematical learning difficulties.
- Explain how these factors can be investigated.
- Explore their impact on learning.
- Discuss and provide a range of tests ranging from pre-requisite skills such as working memory to a critique of normative tests for mathematics knowledge and skills.

The book guides the reader in the interpretation of tests, emphasising the need for a clinical approach when assessing individuals, and shows how diagnosis and assessment can become part of everyday teaching. This resource also includes pragmatic tests which can be implemented in the classroom, and shows how identifying the barriers is the first step in setting up any programme of intervention.

It includes the following:

- Dyscalculia checklist.
- Observation sheet.
- Short-term and working memory test.
- 60-second test for addition and subtraction.

- 120-second test for multiplication and division.
- Maths anxiety assessment.
- 15-minute maths test.
- Test of cognitive style in maths.
- Word problems.

FULL DIAGNOSTIC ASSESSMENT

A full diagnostic assessment for dyscalculia can be carried out by a specialist assessor or an educational psychologist. A range of standardised tests will need to be administered in order to ascertain whether the underlying difficulty is indeed dyscalculia or whether there is a different cause. Tests to assess verbal and visual IQ, working memory and processing speed should all be administered. These quantitative assessments need to be interpreted alongside more qualitative assessments so that a complete picture of the learner's profile can be seen. For example, factors such as maths anxiety, educational history, family history and developmental milestones should be considered.

It is worth bearing in mind the cost of these assessments and the potential benefit to the child. A full dyscalculia diagnosis can be a lengthy and costly exercise. Many learners will respond well to high-quality, specifically tailored intervention from suitably qualified teachers. So, as long as the learner's strengths and weaknesses have been recognised it should be possible to plan a detailed intervention programme that will meet their specific needs. If extra time will help, then a diagnostic assessment would be useful in applying for extra time in statutory exams, particularly if the child has poor processing speed.

EXAM PROVISIONS

Learners and young people in the UK who are identified as having SEN or SpLD are entitled to access arrangements and reasonable adjustments during exams. These adjustments range from additional time in exams to the provision of a scribe/reader or computer-based assistance.

Details of these adjustments are published each year by the Joint Council for Qualifications (JCQ) and are freely available online.

USEFUL WEBSITES

- www.dyscalculiaassociation.uk.
- www.stevechinn.co.uk.
- www.judyhornigold.co.uk.

The three websites above offer information and advice on dyscalculia. The Dyscalculia Association was set up by the author and Steve Chinn in 2018.

- www.patoss-dyslexia.org.
- www.bda-dyslexia.org.uk.

These are two of the larger organisations that offer support and advice for learners with SEND.

- www.mathematicalbrain.com.

This is the website of Professor Brian Butterworth and has links to his research, articles and publications. Ideal if you already have an understanding of dyscalculia.

- www.dyscalculia.org.uk.
- www.dyscalculia.me.uk.
- www.aboutdyscalculia.org.
- www.dyscalculia-Maths-difficulties.org.uk.

The above four websites offer general advice and information about dyscalculia, including checklists, links to other websites and book recommendations.

- www.muliplicationrules.co.uk.

This is a fun and engaging approach to learning the times tables.

- www.ronitbird.co.uk/games.

This is an excellent website for games and ideas. It is aimed at teachers but useful for parents too.

- www.nrich.Maths.org.

This website has hundreds of maths games and activities aimed at both primary and secondary teachers.

- www.addacus.co.uk.
- www.dynamomaths.co.uk.

RECOMMENDED BOOKS

BY THE AUTHOR

- *Can I Tell You About Dyscalculia?* (2020) Jessica Kingsley Publishers.

A book written from the perspective of a primary-aged child with dyscalculia.

- *Making Maths Visual and Tactile* (2016) SENbooks.

Full of ideas for games and activities, aimed at primary teachers but used by many parents of dyscalculic learners.

- *Dyscalculia Pocketbook* (2015) Teacher's Pocketbooks.

A good explanation of dyscalculia for those wanting to further their understanding.

- *Dyscalculia Lesson Plans Books 1 and 2* (2014) Special Direct.

These two books are aimed at teachers planning intervention lessons for learners with dyscalculia.

- *Understanding Maths Learning Difficulties* (2018) Open University Press.

This book is aimed at professionals who are seeking a qualification in dyscalculia and maths difficulties.

BY OTHER AUTHORS

The following books will support dyscalculia-friendly teaching practices. The main message is to make sure that you are supporting your teaching with appropriate concrete manipulatives such as base-10 materials, Cuisenaire rods, dot cards, Numicon, etc.

- *The Trouble with Maths: A Practical Guide to Helping Learners with Numeracy Difficulties* by Steve Chinn (2004) Routledge Falmer.
- *More Trouble with Maths: A Complete Guide to Identifying and Diagnosing Mathematical Difficulties* by Steve Chinn (2012) Routledge.
- *Maths Learning Difficulties, Dyslexia and Dyscalculia* by Steve Chinn (2018) BDA.
- *Dyscalculia Guidance: Helping Pupils with Specific Learning Difficulties in Maths* by Brian Butterworth and Dorian Yeo (2004) nfer Nelson.
- *The Dyscalculia Assessment* by Jane Emerson and Patricia Babtie (2013) Bloomsbury.
- *The Dyscalculia Solution* by Jane Emerson and Patricia Babtie (2014) Bloomsbury.
- *Understanding Dyscalculia and Numeracy Difficulties* by Patricia Babtie and Jane Emerson (2015) Jessica Kingsley.
- *Dyscalculia Toolkit: Supporting Learning Difficulties in Maths* by Ronit Bird (2013) Sage Publications Ltd.
- *The Dyscalculia Resource Book* by Ronit Bird (2011) Sage Publications Ltd.
- *Teaching Maths Creatively* by Linda Pound and Trisha Lee (2021) Routledge.

OTHER RESOURCES

SEN Books (www.senbooks.co.uk).

- Making Maths Visual and Tactile Toolkit.

This is a box of equipment to complement the book of the same title.

- DANS Solutions One.
- DANS Solutions Two.

These two resources are toolkits of ideas and activities for maths difficulties and dyscalculia aimed at learners in Key Stage 1 and Key Stage 2.

TTS

- Dyscalculia Lesson Plans Kit.
- Dyscalculia Games.
- Dyscalculia Problem Solving Cards.
- Two-coloured counters.
- Ten frames.
- Cuisenaire rods.
- Base-10 materials.

FINDEL

- Target Ladders Dyscalculia.
- Addacus.

This is a great resource for teaching place value.

APPS

Call Scotland have a wheel of iPad apps for learners with dyscalculia and numeracy difficulties, which can be found here:
www.callscotland.org.uk/common-assets/cm-files/posters/ipad -apps-for-learners-with-dyscalculianumeracy-difficulties.pdf.

IT RESOURCES

I would thoroughly recommend these websites/games for parents as they are fun, engaging and non-threatening. A great way to support your child:

- Nessy numbers: www.nessy.com.uk.
- Number Shark: www.wordshark.co.uk.
- Maths Explained videos by Steve Chinn: www.stevechinn.co.uk.
- Number Sense Games: www.number-sense.co.uk.
- The Number Race: www.thenumberrace.com.
- IDL Numeracy: www.idlsgroup.com/numeracy.
- Dynamo Maths: www.dynamomaths.co.uk.
- Number Gym: www.numbergym.co.uk.
- The Number Catcher: www.thenumbercatcher.co.uk.

CASE STUDIES

The following link details some case studies of people with dyscalculia:

- http://beatdyscalculia.com/tag/beat-dyscalculia-case-studies/
- www.dynamomaths.co.uk/DynamoCaseStudies2.html?sub-menuheader=2.
- https://dyscalculia.advancelearningzone.com/index.php?option=com_content&view=article&id=4&Itemid=4.

PROFESSIONAL TRAINING COURSES

Teachers who are interested in becoming a specialist dyscalculia teacher or dyscalculia assessor can find information about training courses and professional accreditation from:

Dyscalculia Association: www.dyscalculiaassociation.uk.

Level 3 and Level 5 online dyscalculia courses accredited by OCN London.

BDA: www.Bdadyslexia.org.uk.

Level 5 online course accredited by OCN4learning.

Edge Hill University: www.edgehill.ac.uk.

PGCE and Diploma in Dyscalculia.

INDEX

abstraction 36, 76
anxiety: increasing 14; levels 15-16; maths 10, 13-18, 21, 30-31, 64-65, 67-68, 110, 118, 124; mild 15; parental 14, 113; severe 31
assessment 12, 123; diagnostic 122, 124; dynamo 121; informal 122; maths anxiety 124; qualitative 124; quantitative 124

bar model 89, 96, 103-104, 106-108; use of 102, 118
Berteletti, I. 58, 69
Bird, R. 95
British Dyslexia Association (BDA) 3, 119; Dyscalculia Committee 3
Bruner, J. 56, 73
Butterworth, B. 116, 125

cardinality 27, 30, 36, 38-39, 76-77
Chinn, S. 54, 78, 82, 120, 123, 125
communication 44, 59, 69, 117-118
concrete, pictorial, abstract (CPA) approach 56, 66, 73
conservation 30, 36, 53, 77, 85-86, 89
Cuisenaire, G. 90-91
Cuisenaire rods 57, 64, 90, 92, 94-95, 127-128

Dienes blocks 25, 57, 91, 95
dominoes 66, 79
Dorean Yeo pattern 78
Dweck, C. 21
dyscalculia: acquired 10; assessment 122, 124; awareness of 117; causes 9; definition of 3; developmental 3, 7, 12; diagnosis 124; effects of 113; -friendly 65-66, 69, 120; impact of 10-12; indicators of 24; potential 120; prenatal influences 9; prevalence of 13, 29; primary 6; pseudo- 31; screening 7, 121-122; secondary 6; severe 11
Dyscalculia Association 125
dyslexia 6, 11, 29-30, 107
dyspraxia 6, 11

Einstein, A. 55
estimation 49, 51-52, 55, 104, 114; difficulties 55; skills 25, 51

flexibility 20, 24, 51, 55
fluent calculation 3, 5-6
Fragile X syndrome 9

Gattegno, C. 90
generalisation 27, 44, 58-59, 66, 69, 85

Howden, H. 49

inclusion 37

Jackson, E. 17

levels of oral counting 37-38

magnitude comparison 7-8
manipulatives 46, 57, 62-63,
    65-66, 69, 73, 95-96, 108,
    117-118; concrete 25, 61, 73,
    118, 127; continuous 64; use
    of 25, 63-66, 103; versatile
    94; virtual 118
maths development 35, 122
memory 115; auditory 90;
    long-term 6, 59; short-term
    6, 123; spatial 85; visual 81,
    90; working 9-10, 18, 59,
    68, 123-124
metacognition 44-45, 49,
    64, 69
Milner, A. 116
mindset 20-21; fixed 20-21;
    growth 20-21, 30, 111
Mobius, A. 111
Moorcraft, P. 11, 116

neuro-diversity 4, 6, 117
Newman, A. 100-101, 108
Newman's Procedure
    100, 104
number: bonds 27, 40, 42,
    84, 90, 94; conservation
    of 30, 36, 77, 85-86, 89,
    decomposing 27; facts 3,
    5, 27, 90; manipulation
    of 13, 24; mental 40-41,
    43; processing of 9;
    recomposing 5, 27;
    relationships 5, 90, 121;
    sense 3-7, 12, 24, 28, 44,
    49-51, 55, 64, 69, 84, 86,

89-90, 113, 121; symbol 4;
    system 4, 24, 35, 67, 75,
    77, 85, 110, 120; see also
    patterns
Numicon 79, 82, 117, 127;
    patterns 82; tiles 66

Open University 55

patterns 26, 57, 59, 63-64,
    66, 71, 78, 91, 114; dice 66,
    82; dot 9, 24, 40, 66, 77,
    80; number 77-78; random
    82; see also Numicon
Pavlovian response 15
Pelmanism 85
Polya, G. 100

Ramful, A. 57
Rose review (2009) 45
rounding 54-55

Schwartz, L.-M. 19
Sharma, M. 5, 60-61, 73
Singapore approach 73
somatosensory 58
spatial awareness 6
stroop effect 7
subitising 3, 7-8, 12, 23-24,
    28, 38, 80, 83, 114;
    conceptual 8-9, 39, 41,
    80-84; perceptual 8, 39,
    41, 80-81

timed tests 18
transition 42, 96 110
Turner's syndrome 9

unitising 37

visualisation 41, 44, 54-58,
    65, 69, 75, 85, 90

Williams syndrome 9

Printed in the United States
by Baker & Taylor Publisher Services